THE ROSEBUD VARIATIONS

DeWald

I0149140

ISBN: 978-1-913642-63-1

Book designed by Aaron Kent

Edited by Aaron Kent

Broken Sleep Books (2021), Talgarreg, Wales

Contents

For Kali

The Rosebud Variations

Jaydn DeWald

They all dreamt of each other that night, as was natural,
considering how thin the partitions were between them . . .
—Virginia Woolf

Pastoral Noir: 7 Paragraphs

1.

If I knew my father was rotting in some desolate little nursing home, I might consider looking for him. Then again, if I could find a dead cockroach in the bottom of my coffee thermos, as I did this morning, I suppose I could find him ageless and beatific—maybe tearing a four-wheeler through a field of mist. I once believed that if I could find my father in my imagination— *What if I found him slurping oysters on the porch of a powder-blue mansion?*—then there'd be no need to look for him. I once believed, too, that if I did my mother's laundry, I could find (in the bottom of her sock drawer) a photograph of him manning a shrimp boat in a gale, so that if I lifted the socks, I could taste the electricity in the air, I could touch the bones in his face, I could smell his aftershave and his sweat. Now, however, it seems best for me to ignore the imagination: the poor kid bagging my groceries, if he happens to resemble me, is not my long-lost brother, for example. Indeed, if I hadn't this desire to find my father in a wheelchair under a fungus-ridden oak, as in an old Bergman film, I might not think about him at all anymore— about finding him, and thence abandoning him, in a vastness of wind-eroded stone. Even so, there appears to be a gulf between the mind and the world of action—my father, even if he'd abandoned me in person, had not necessarily abandoned me in spirit—therefore I begin to resort to my old habits: *What if I found him calling me across a lake on a sapphirine morning? What if his own imagination, like an arm of charcoal smoke, was reaching for me?*

2.

I believe my girlfriend may be playing for somebody else in the audience. Her face, when lifted, seems to drift toward the middle-back row of seats. However, I must admit that the auditorium is quite dark—the audience is just a bundle of silhouettes—and she could, therefore, be playing for me while looking at somebody else, a silhouette that perhaps resembles me. Worse things have happened. Indeed, once, on a train, my wheelchair got lodged between two seats, and two big porters had to lug me along the aisle and to the toilet. Nonetheless, I think: *Why should I get her song and not her eyes?* For the same reason she gets your mind and not your body, I tell myself. My girlfriend bows her head. I cannot bow my head because she may, while I'm not looking, lift her face to—well, to whom seems to matter little anymore. I must admit that I have been playing with myself again: she will no longer be coming home with me. She will linger on, here, with the cocktail-toting crowd. Her eyebrows rise. Her fingers sprinkle among the high keys. Yet I believe she may know that I am here: I am the only silhouette, after all, sitting in the red-carpeted aisle, pretending to conduct her.

3.

The boy who is afraid of death lives for dreams.
—Hideo Furukawa

Last night, on a whim, I rented this Swedish art-house film in which a middle-aged man, waking from a long nap, finds himself sitting across from his dead mother in a rowboat. "Unbelievable," I said, watching the man lean in to embrace her, the ghost of her, though his arms whooshed right through her and he tumbled forward against the gunwale. The whole scene, down to the old woman's olive-green slickers, had an uncanny resemblance to a dream: there, in that same rowboat, had I tried and failed to embrace my own mother, who I'd only seen, until then, in photographs (a sleepy-eyed woman behind a curtain of sunlit, windblown hair). Had the haggard figure on the screen also committed suicide, plunging, as my mother had, from a metal bridge in her red kimono? Water lapped against the hull. I watched the man watch his mother stare through him into the braided mist as if he should find the answer there. Then the piccolo began—as it had in my dream—as I had known it would, all along—like the quivering of a slender stem upon a mountain. I remembered her arms around my head. White light through a white sheet, the violet nipple coming near. As the old woman stood listening to the distant flute, so I stood listening in the auroral greenness of my living room, proffering my hand. "Mother," I said, reaching through the screen, hoisting her up out of the rowboat and into my home. "There," I said. There. Gripping my hand, gazing at me from under the hood of her dripping slicker, my mother, who smelled like wind high in the gilded treetops, sat me down on my futon and then, dragging back her hood, began to tell me . . .

4.

Dorothy tapped her heels together & woke up in Kansas again. Once, at the height of winter, I hitchhiked from Athens, Georgia, to New Brunswick, New Jersey, coughing up little blood-flecked pebbles of I don't know what—my heart? Now we find ourselves in a field of towering sunflowers not unlike those old Mombi set before Tip & his gang in *The Marvelous Land of Oz* (1904): "a girl's face in the center of each flower." Why did I leave X, whose face (doe-eyed, flushed with wine, staring into a bowl of cold cioppino) I can still see through a steamed-up restaurant window, late summer, 1993? We must be stuffed with experience, the way the Scarecrow's stuffed with straw (or money), able to reach inside ourselves, ferret around, then wrench out this or that humiliating moment—as when, on a booze cruise, one stabbed an escargot fork into one's forearm, pledging one's love to a total stranger. Dorothy was seven when she first came to Oz. Did she ever grow up, menstruate ("develop," Aunt Em might say), kneel down in the dust for a lanky farm boy? For a split second I'm carrying her in my arms—a heroic father—through the sunflowers, through the emerald pesticides & the wind. But it's just a hallucination. Tap your Adidas together & wake up in Z's tenement again, mid-to-late autumn, San Francisco, 2007, staring up at a storm-gray staircase (I was singing & would soon be carried away myself, I now remember) sweeping ever upward into blackness, into a little skylight of night, like a twister—

5.

"The garden is here in the middle of your bedroom," the beau-model whispers, unbuttoning his mandarin orange blouse, then raising his arms in the manner of—the painter thinks—the Spaniard before Napoleon's firing squad. The painter steps toward him and lifts the blouse over his head. Kisses his shoulder. Kisses his firm, café au lait chest. *The Third of May 1808.* Goya was, at the time of composition, a deaf widower living with his housemaid in Madrid. With the flat of his hand, the model pushes the painter back onto the bed. He kneels between the painter's legs and begins to undo his belt . . . And the painter wonders if Goya had, before his stroke in Bordeaux, looked affectionately back upon his old pain in the silent metropolis, searching for pleasure as for a blotch of darkness among the tomatoes and grapes and pure Andalusian horses. The beau gathers up his black hair and buns it. Takes the painter into his mouth and, a bit roughly, pulls his testicles. "I see only forms that are lit up and forms that are not," said Goya. The painter remembers—then chooses to ignore—the mark of stigmata on the Spaniard's right palm. With eyes half closed, he sees the silver, early-nineteenth-century moonlight swimming through the model's hair.

6.   after Yasunari Kawabata

The harbor town is chockfull of mothers: for each guest at the inn, there is a mother who will stay with him. From the instant he wakes to the post-lunch stroll along the docks to the quiet, meditative hour in the wicker deck chair, watching the sun sink like a blazing Japanese fan into the ocean, she is at his side. And yet when he asks her, at the rustic cafeteria tables, amidst the steam of his clam chowder, to return home and live with him, she tilts her head and says: "Ohh, sweetie, I can only be your mother here, for a little while, okay?" It's then he realizes—something in her voice perhaps?—that she is more than a mere presence, a sheer silhouette beside him onto which he can project his remembered mother: she is, indeed, a rather gaunt and gray-faced woman, in a white cotton dress and brown cashmere sweater, like a nurse, teary-eyed after the loss of a patient. "Every morning I take the elevator down to the lobby and believe I will find my son here," she tells him. "But there are only ever middle-aged men in wrinkled Polo shirts, looking lost and frightened." He puts an arm around her: she has begun to cry. "Now now," he says. "You're still my mother. You have bright red hair, which sunlight turns to fire, and a miniature setting moon in each of your fingernails." He gently pulls her up from the table. It's time for their walk. He will not let himself think about packing his suitcase, or returning the persimmon-colored keycard to the concierge, or standing out on the deck of the lowing steamer, one of a hundred other guests, each waving through the grainy predawn mist to his mother. "Cloudlike hands on my fever-ish forehead," he says, ushering her toward the mechanical glass-doored exit. "Pitcher of iced tea and your quiet humming." She gazes down at the tiled floor, silent, and the doors slide open. "Gold bracelets tinkling the length of your forearm. Don't you remember?" he says, as together they enter the stream of mother-son pairs strolling arm in arm along the promenade, as together they become indistinguishable from the others ...

7.

We see the man standing on the corner of 24th and Mission, hailing a cab, then again on the wet piers, under an iron lamp, looking out to sea. Still later, watching *Brazil*, we see him standing in the street outside our window, staring at us under his hatbrim, so we close the curtains, lock the deadbolts, and turn off all the lights in the house. After a few minutes, we unpause the film, but we can no longer concentrate: we are concerned about the man, that he may reveal something about our lives, our pasts, that he has come here to unravel us. We crawl into bed, silent, and listen to footfalls that, though distant, seem to explode right in our ears. *Are they the man's footfalls? Should we pull aside the curtain and see?* We cannot decide: we lie here, too frightened to move, though filled with the desire to know. We sense that one of us may soon summon the courage to peek out the window, leaving the other alone, but we do not let on. We even fling off the silk sheets for a swift separation; still, neither of us moves. The one who leaves our bed does not believe in our union, and we believe in our union. Let the man pace all night under the orange streetlamps, in the gathering fog: he is not a part of us; he cannot determine our fate. We listen to the lowing of the cargo ships, then to the gaggle of bar-goers on Clement Street playing "Marco Polo," then finally—ominously—to the footfalls again. Though we long to know what the other is thinking, what the other has been hiding all these years, we find ourselves reaching out across the bedspread, as across an impossible expanse, to squeeze each other's hand.

Arrangement, Nuclear

We discovered our house was spheroid, like the earth.

Our beds were afloat on moonlit carpets.

Our daughter feverishly drawing circles in black crayon on butcher paper—did she think she was stirring a potion, generating a storm?

I used to write poems ending with lone boats creaking at sundown.

All winter we perched on stools in our garage, piecing together scorched-edged shreds of a map.

Our son gently pulled our eyelashes, or he squirmed his hands inside our mouths as though we were sock puppets.

Suddenly a dark wave of laundry crashed over us.

I closed my eyes, I listened to womb noises, I tasted burnt toast in the air.

Like the earth, too, our house was rotating.

My partner wore a long sheer nightgown that she swished around and around until she disappeared—

Past Developing

Forget the waitress who resembled Sappho.

Between the tines of our forks. On the tube

But even that light made her cheeks glisten.

And raised the centuries-old wine that had

Suit I wore in college—the darkness inside.

To which Odysseus had been tied. And yet

Via video surveillance. Our hunk of peasant

We carried around our necks huge Polaroid

Through red window curtains, light caught

On the specials chalkboard, the old barman

The salt cod she served us drifted like sand

Sat children painting little clay St. Jeromes,

"I'm greener than the grass is green," I said,

Our heads spinning. I dreamt of the Gorilla

Behind the bar stood the rotted, black mast

Its placard: *None of this is being preserved*

Bread. Those paper placemats. Plates of oil.

Cameras, so there was no use remembering.

Us red-handed, napkins rising to our noses.

Playing Hangman. One leg. No I's. No face.

Round Midnight

Back seat of a train car   the black water rush
Of night   outside the windows   watching you
Pick your cuticles   over a battered blue-
And-yellow paperback   *On Meditation*
As you in a whisper   almost a hiss   explain
That for us to have remained   that static-misty winter
Together   would have   like an animal
Like a frenzied creature   shoved again and
Again into its dirt tunnel   killed you
That was why   I arrived home mid-   afternoon
Cloudlight through sheer curtains   barges
Lowing in the bay   to a bedroom pillaged
A few crumpled garments   sweat-grayed panties
On the floor   and now   slowly from your fore-
Finger   a beadlet of blood   falls
Onto the book cover   which you instantly
Wipe   with your green knit scarf and at which
Years later   I will gaze   sliding the slim volume
From our shelf   in the shadow-latticed hall
A faint russet streak   I will press
To the tip of my tongue   the way one
Tests a battery   for tingling   and still I am
Here beside you   in the flickering
Fluorescent train lights   like a man lost
Inside a monstrous costume   watching his hands
Unbodied   through two   too distant eye-
Holes   sweep strands of hair from
Your forehead   so that I   without touching you
Can touch you   pull you   against my chest
That shared wall   thick with damp fur
Inside me   on the other side of which I eaves-
Drop on my own life   and on you
Verily gasping out   a volley of apologies
Into the heart   of my liver-   purple sweater
Though my propensity   for silent reflection
For standing   unblinking   at the kitchen sink

Just holding a grease-smeared enamel plate   and remembering
Some childhood   morning with its blond light
Lighting the blond hair   of my inner thighs
As "Round Mid-   night" crackled on the turntable
Must have contributed   to your leaving
To your deep   zero-gravity sleep in some-
Body else's red cotton sheets   dreaming of insects
I want to believe   when in fact you'd told me
Already   over lattes and burnt pancakes
In shabby Empire chairs   that in those three
Soft-focus months with-   out me
You had become less a person   than a thing
A body of wind   sewn   into the very air
A dream   of invisibility   and so
I stand suddenly   like the captain of a ship
In the bow   riding the black river   of night
And yank the bell cord   because this is our
Stop   and we need to walk   home together
Arm in   arm against the cold-wet   wind
I   the husband   you need me
To pretend to be   leading us down the train's steps
And out into darkness   the orange-brown
Pools of street-   lamps *On Meditation*
Slipped in my left rear   trouser pocket   a coward-
Hero   still silent   still unblinking
Taking your chewed-up   finger into my mouth

Sonnet Granadas

for Bill Evans

Six chords, then silence, then the world
  Was made. Just like my heart in its feeble
Birdcage. It was autumn. I listened with
  Eyes closed. Light strobing among leaves,

The phonograph crackling and popping
  As if your *Trio with Symphony Orchestra*
Was burning, Bill, right in the fireplace.

  Stone angel, little deep-thinking statuette—
I was the dragonfly lighted in your hair,
  I was the moss around your demure ankle.

A huddle of grass shivering as if afraid.
  Tell me, Bill. How did you do all of that?
How'd you make the yellow leaves fall,
  The pond, in slow motion, ripple inward?

Acting, Method

Once, on stage, a boy became
    My Father. I knelt before him
And he placed two fish bones

On my tongue. Rank, delicate
    Little bones. Our blue skyline

Rustled. Two choirboys, each
    On a white cloud, rode by me
Laughing & jerking overhead.

It was a beautiful age to learn
    Pain. One could walk, sunsets,

In orange pastures, venting to
    One's boring donkey. Gazing
So often into the black mouth

Of a well—one was forced to
    Consider Death. Three priests

Started (stage left) to feed me
    Lines: *His body is home now.*
His body is at home, I said &

Munched those little bones to
    Sand. My Father stared down

Repulsed or stunned or afraid.
    In rolled a backdrop of purple
Mountains. Then a single girl

In a red tutu, spinning around
    Like a small, overzealous fire.

The Reward of Cruelty

Had we the odor of summer, of the gazillion pine-needle dresses
Jiggling from the boughs, when the Hogarth, tacked above the register, lured us in
  Among the bookshelves, the golden motes of dust? Um, well, no—
Though we'd made it in the park, in some out-of-bounds shadows, and would find,
  Later that evening, a peppering of aphids in your hair. We stared
At the Hogarth. *The reward of cruelty.* Nero on the dissection table, his intestines
  Slopped into a pail. Still, it didn't seem as dark as this, in person—
What with Mingus on the stereo, the sienna light of late afternoon, of a childhood
  Among hay-bales and languid figures—didn't it seem, in person,
Tranquil, like a dish of cream? You reached for Nero, leaning against the counter,
Revealing the pale bell of your hips, while I trudged, in my head,
  Down the sun-baked trails of Sausalito, where your grandmother lived, and where,

Months before, in the rip-gut brome, I'd found a raccoon's skull

As pale as a breast. But back to you, dear, reaching for Nero, for the gaping mouth,

So that I may recall myself, beneath you, in the wardrobe mirror—

My own gasping, fishlike mouth against your pillows. Then you looked back at me

Over your shoulder, a doe in silver mist, liable to leap away

At the slightest movement. Could you even appreciate how silent my silence was,

How I stood there as still as a prisoner, as a glass of water, while

You examined me—the insides of me, it seemed—the white mutt, in the Hogarth,

Lowering its jowls, all this time, round Nero's heart on the floor?

Round Midnight (2)

i lie
  sleepless

for a few
  minutes

then return
  to my partner

washing
  my face

in a huge pail
  of water

on which
  the red moon

sparkles
  down her

white
  forearms

but i know
  i am sleeping

i can hear
  outside

my tent
  the white-

tailed fawn
  rolling

my ripe
  cantaloupe

with her
  black muzzle

toward her
  warm place

in the leaves
  & needles

The Hammock

My neighbor hung a hammock   from the porch
    Of his solid glass mansion,   so that whenever a sleepy passerby
Decided to snooze there   (it was late October, & yellow
    Orange red updrafts of leaves   —miniature tornados—
Would appear to entrance folks   & lead them
    Straight toward it)   he could strut   buck naked across the transparent
Floor overhead,   enticing her or him   to come upstairs.
    Just yesterday,   watching from my study window
Across the street, I was nearly   enticed to wander over there
    Myself—I'd already   buttoned to the throat   my red
Flannel mackinaw—   when I saw a woman thinly reflected
    In glass   all around her, circling   his hammock the way
One might circle   a small Italian sports car. Meanwhile,
    My neighbor approached her   as soundless as a spider
From above . . .   Gradually, ungripping my lace curtain,
    I saw that the woman   was dressed like me—stone-
washed jeans & sneakers & the red   flannel mackinaw—as though

She were *my* reflection & it was I   circling the hammock
Running two fingers   along its crisply folded edge. Resolved
    To go out there, to be at last   with my reflections, I started
Toward the door,   though scarcely had I taken half a step
    When a shrill yowl   exploded from without,   & I spun
Back to the window: there,   above the hammock, above
    My doppelgänger's head,   a peacock with fanned
Iridescent plumage   yowled & strutted in a tight semi-   circle,
    & again yowled & strutted & then   yowled again; & the woman,
In response, raised her hands   palm outward   & slowly
    Backed down the porch . . .   Already
I was lumbering out my door,   never mind that my neighbor
    Had disappeared or else   metamorphosed into a peacock. Already
I was in the center of my lawn,   slashing my bare hands
    Through a tornado   of red orange yellow leaves that—
Like the static rustling   of a TV—   blotted out
    His entire mansion. Then   just as swiftly darkness fell, the leaves
Settled at my feet, & I stood there   at the border
    Of our adjoined yards   as though I was still at my window, still
A mere shadow   behind pink lace. I gazed up
    At my neighbor's porch   now thronged with uniformed
Police officers (& their   reflections) strobing eerily

Red & blue, no   sound at all, in their cruisers'
Lightbars. Five or six of them   rushed toward me: I didn't—
    Couldn't—move. Roughly   I was lifted into the air & conveyed,
Crowd-surf-style,   onto the porch, where five or six others
Hip-   thrusting to music I could only   now hear thumping
Faintly beyond the glass walls   commenced to tug
    At the sleeves   of my mackinaw & to untuck
My lime green   button-up. In seconds   they had me shirt-
less, & were about to   start in (to my very literal
Excitement) on my jeans,   when a voice barked: *Stop!*
& onto the porch   strode my neighbor, buck naked,
Smeared with their watery   red-&-blues. I stepped   backward; I saw
    Myself—or was it   another doppelgänger?—in the reflection
In the glass, sprinting   up the street,   just as the woman had,
    Though I remained   on the porch, sensing the hammock
Behind me the way one   might sense
    A hole in the earth. *Is it mystery,   the unknown, you are after?*
Asked my neighbor,   backing me up
    Against the hammock.   *Sexual transcendence?* He tilted his head
Questioningly. *Love?* Some-   body had unzipped
    My jeans, which now slid   to my ankles: I almost tripped.
Yes, I said. *All   of those things. Yes.* Where-

upon he slipped   from his dense   thatch of pubic hair
A long   iridescent peacock feather & at once
Brushed it—its turquoise eye   stared at me—in wide arcs
Across my chest, as though tracing   a symbol. Then:
You too must sleep, he said. Meaning   the world
Isn't good enough.   *Don't worry—   I'll wake you.*
I'll wake   all of you, I heard him say   as I fell back
Into the hammock, fell back   into the feathered
Darkness   of sleep & am still   falling . . .

In Space Things Touch. In Time Things Part

You can't stick a string quintet
Under a Japanese maple, expecting to attract the piano teacher

On an evening stroll. Haven't you seen Spielberg's latest flick,
The one where insectile robots

Sneak under our bathroom doors? Of course not. You've been
Hopping islands again, like Odysseus, minus all the adventure

And one-night stands. To think
I'd fallen, as a teenager, for the tortuous wiring of your bonsai—

Your spiderlike fingers bending a slender bough. Look around,
Kid. Hasn't the theater changed:

Your slipper tub overflowing, your black guitar case crammed
With dead moths? The piano teacher, on the leaf-stippled path,

Requires more than a sport coat
Spread across some shade; never mind that you're posed there

In your undies, gnawing grilled squid. Too late for firecrackers,
Even the elegant popping ones

That tend to announce a wooing. You'll have to schlepp home
Buck naked through the woods, stepping from light to shadow,

From shadow to light, et cetera,
Brimming, like a wineglassful of milk, with desire. Marvelous,

Isn't it: to watch your decisions unfold, as on an IMAX screen,
And to simply shrug at the fool

You'll soon be, and are? White moons in the yellowing leaves
Of the footpath. And look: here she comes, arousing analogies

Between gardenias and the bra
Peeking out of her sleeveless top. The rest, well, is predictable—

Like when a spaceship explodes, and a villain spirals, howling,
Into a galactic void. In no time,

Your string quintet's trilling over the treetops, filling the night,
Though the piano teacher, turning, swinging his peroxide hair,

Has spotted you: naked, lucent,
Dangling a ragged squid over your open mouth. Will he arise

From his piano bench some evening, late in life, recalling you
(Poor thing) there in the woods,

As he stares through a dark window, contemplates the grapes
On his Formica counter? You, kid, have the sublimest dreams—

Too bad you can't live in them.

Voyage Out

He's standing beside his hammock, above his sleeping body, which dreams of stumbling along an ever-winding path of leaves & ashes, when a distant, quavering soprano begins to sing—a voice he'd heard, years before, on a bronze hill overlooking the ocean, & ever since regretted not searching for, not hurtling toward her in the rubescent dusk of summer, tearing off his rucksack. "Wake up," he tells his body, nudging its shoulder with his knee. But it goes on lying there, like an enormous baby in a sling, because it is dying in its sleep: it has collapsed on the dark path among the scraping leaves, watching his twelve-year-old daughter in her plum-black dress (so like a dream within a dream) stumble forward in its place. He runs his hand over the blond hairs of its forearm. Then he stares up at the white light through the lemon trees & at his daughter dancing, one rainy evening, before the old projector, the old faces of relatives (contorted, celery-green) streaked across her flannel PJs. What can account for this desire to hurtle out into the streets, to find the soprano's voice, rising again, in the paling distance? *Art thou a little spirit bearing up a corpse*, as Epictetus said, or is the soprano tempting him—like an egret on a thin branch—to leave, to let the body go? His daughter, at the beach with some friends, in the tarantualic shadow of a palm tree, will no doubt walk, hours later, over the damp grass toward his body, then suddenly freeze in the middle of the yard—warm & windless & the moon in her salt-hardened hair—noticing a smudge of white, the peak of his nose, above the hammock. Now he's touching for the last time (as his daughter will, crumpling to her knees) the paper eyelids, the colorless lips & ill-shaven chin. O how he's dreamt of the soprano silhouetted on an ice floe, of lurching toward her through rags of swirling snow, burning to see her, to watch her sing! Soon his daughter, as she replaced his body in its dream, will be standing right here in this place before the hammock, trying again & again to shape these wooden fingers around her tiny hand—although by then, of course, he will be long gone, loping across violet sands, searching for the soprano: the quavering voice, the painted mouth . . .

Triad

I am sequestered in the greenhouse again, pensive,
    Snipping little branches. He (my son) has no need

    To search for me, as he used to. See? His window
Is open; he is practicing Schumann, *Kinderszenen,*

Op. 15, a way of calling to me. But I won't budge.
    She may be with him, like a terrible nun / gripping

A black stick. Hah—if that were true, I would not
    Have left the chicken, beheaded, in the white sink

    To cower among marigolds. Her stupid / naïveté
Terrifies me: at any moment, I feel she may utter:

    I love your father. Or, worse: *We love each other.*
        Thus the shears trembling in my pale hands. Thus

I could snip my manhood. Beyond the glass walls,
    Light caught in the bare tree; my son approaching

    The fourth piece, "Pleading Child," with his green
Drapes billowing. I feel I shouldn't be / permitted

    Such beauty. My gorged flowers hang their heads.
        Son: I want you to hear how Horowitz played this

In Hamburg, June, 1987—the album's by my bed—
    But shame, like a horrendous crashing of the keys,

    Stoops me forward. Here, tormented, I will remain.
I am your father, I can never / allow myself to heal.

Landscape with Sashimi

Yoshi's Jazz Club & Japanese Restaurant
—San Francisco, April 2008

his birthday   he's drunk   he keeps

ramming his bell against the mic   still

he tries to scream   to shred   I mean

to simply tear it up, man   like he did

on *First Light*   1971   with Hancock

Henderson   Carter   Benson

DeJohnette & so on   but he's

a different player   a different person

now   his solo   a flock of ungainly

tin birds scattering pell-mell   he can

only stand there grumbling   fiddling

with his valves   after a few measures

of nothing   Hutcherson bursts in

four-malleted   open-mouthed   &

Freddie whips around   as though to

make him listen   respectful   head

bowed   should I storm out   hop in

my olive-green Saab   blast *Hub Tones*

& forget it all   the whole evening

the audience hollering   *Red Clay! Little*

Sunflower!   Yesterday's Dreams!   Well

there he is   the Hub of Hubbard

slumped on his stool   defeated   one

hand fondling the fat   pink child

of his underlip Oh   come on, Freddie

give it up   we forgive   your drinking

your chops   even your hubris   still

know this   I will not be the one white

strait-   laced person   who tries to

describe your prowess   to the poor

young   oblivious waitress   leaning

over my table   handing me my dish of

lugubrious   *uni*

Notes for Winter

I don't forget   you're not here anymore
Stepping out of the bath   like a white shadow

As I drop   handfuls of ripped letters
From our bedroom window   bright snow-words

Tumbling in the night   in the streetlight
Whereas once   I walked beside you

Among houseboats   patched and barnacled
Wind in our loose clothes   now I stand

In the mirror   beyond our unlit rooms
At the end of the corridor   like a young boy waiting

For a dance   I know these little scraps of letters
Don't tornado whitely   upward together

Against the green night   to form your body
Darkward they tumble   then wink out

In silence   beneath my hand in mid-gesture
Almost grasping palm-outward   still air

The Rosebud Variations

Then a rain-soaked rosebud appears
—Reuben Jackson

Round ten o'clock at night, I entered Szechuan Gardens—a cavernous, red-curtained Chinese restaurant—one of our favorites—overcome with the preposterous sensation that I was late, that she was there at one of the shadowy tables, rapping her knuckles, waiting for me . . . Outside, a light rain slanted through the floating orange-brown orbs of the streetlamps and, walking under them, repeating to myself the sentence, "For me, my mother made up fairy tales"—a spur-of-the-moment addition to the sniveling eulogy I'd delivered that afternoon over my mother's casket—repeating this sentence, I had at some point lowered my umbrella and just let it bounce dumbly against my leg. I must have looked hideous, standing there in the dark-veined marble foyer of the Gardens, mascara-streaked, dripping wet, like a little battered rowboat come to port. But who the hell cares? I needed our meal: wonton soup, pan-fried dumplings, Kung Pao chicken, a pot of oolong tea. I clanked my wet umbrella into the aluminum bucket just inside the door, and four red-shirted waitresses playing cards at a table across the room looked up at me, then back down at their hands. Slowly, a chair was scraped back. I raised my index finger. I said—I wanted to try out the phrase—I said: "Just one."

The minute I'd been seated at our familiar small round Formica table, I began to ferret around in my purse. I was certain that my mother's fairy tales, if I did not write them down, would be lost forever. Why did I also think of our trip to Bogotá almost a decade earlier? On the banks of Lake Guatavita, our tour guide had explained over his cheap, squawking loudspeaker that Muisca chieftains, sprayed with gold dust, annually paddled out to the middle of this lake and there, glistening in the first light as though with urine or clarified butter, as offering to a golden goddess dove in and washed themselves in the dawn-reflecting water. Was it because the tradition proved ephemeral? Was it because my mother, smoothing my hair in our flower-wallpapered hotel room, a muted soccer match playing on the TV, told me one of her tales over a bottle of Aguardiente? Or maybe I once thought death was like that: one lost one's sheen, one's idol-like luster, but was reborn humbler and truer and more revealed. Anyway, I was certain there was a little black dime-store notebook in here somewhere. Ahh, here it is. And a pen? Yes, my cheap blue Bic pen from Bank of America: perfect. Now let's see. There was, I remembered, a particularly memorable fairy tale about a fisherman's daughter—a variation, I would discover later, reading at a patio table outside Boudin Bakery, dunking slices of French baguette into clam chowder—a variation of a fairy tale called "The Rosebud" that the Brothers Grimm and a slew of others have transcribed or translated, often with significant liberties. Still, truth be told, I had little to no interest in transcriptions, translations, variations, liberties, or even quality. However romantic or naïve or sentimental it may be, I simply wanted to live inside my mother. I wanted to feel what she felt, think what she thought, know what she knew, dream what she dreamed, in the act of composition.

🌹

There was once a poor fisherman whose daughter walked to the beach every afternoon to gather seashells. Whereupon she might have thought: a fairy tale is a straight and narrow path; to follow it and no others, the teller must be disciplined. Hence, the daughter's collection of shells arranged on a black velvet jeweler's cloth is an indulgent detail, not to mention personal: my mother possessed just such a collection on a shelf above her bed and, one languid pink morning, rolling them one by one in her paper-skin palm as though to activate her memory, the loose hospital bracelet—aren't they supposed to remove those?—still hanging round her thin bruised tremoring wrist, seemed intent on describing the origin (the beach, her company, the time of day) of each small and ordinary shell. Yet by the second shell—this one was plucked from Stinson Beach during a hopeless quest for a girlfriend's silver stud earrings—my mother would stop midsentence and, heaving a sigh, turn her heavy-lidded gaze to the window as to the dullest interlocutor in the world. I stood. I began to gather up the seashells from her lap. I told her to get some rest.

She didn't respond. But no matter. Being a disciplined teller, I think I'll leave us there, in that sickroom, with me at her bedside, and the salmon light streaming through her see-through cloud of hair: no need to expand upon or luxuriate in trivialities. Does it matter that I would, the following morning, remembering that policemen had lain straw on the sidewalk outside Arnold Bennett's window, so that the sound of foot traffic would not disturb the dying novelist—does it matter that I would drape my own mother's walk with old sheets and rags and tees and pillowcases? Of course not. Nothing, after all, is more indulgent than the personal, and a fairy tale is staunchly impersonal, if not ruthlessly cold.

🌹

I had by now stood my leather-bound, cracked-open menu before me on the table, creating in effect a little cubicle in which to write. I wrote: *Once, when she had gone a long way without a single shell, a handsome merman broke the surface of the tide and beckoned her to hop in and look for oysters.* I found it—still find it—fascinating that my mother's introduction to the marvelous, the first appearance of the "handsome merman," is so nonchalant, so casually tossed off, that he might have been, barring his good looks, just another local fisherman, a teenage boy out for a swim, or a canoeist raising a paddle and halloing ashore, especially since she'd been courted as a young woman by a series of handsome, not-so-young men who would remain, until very nearly the end, alive in her memory—little huts forever burning across the raven-dark countryside of her mind. At eighteen, when she traveled to Italy between the wars, my mother met an officer of the Royal Army named Rinaldo or Rolando or Renato—I disremember—a man, in any event, with brown caterpillar eyebrows, tobacco-scented breath ("The aroma of pipesmoke," she once told me, "still makes me bat my lashes") and an officer's cap worn stylishly aslant—a man known chiefly among my mother's intimates as the one who, on a moonlit beach in Tropea, picked strands of seaweed from her wet and clotted hair. She first told me this story in a Macy's changing stall, slinking out of (I could see through the door-slats) a pale green dress, and she told it—how could she resist?—as a love story, a brief romance, a tryst. Still, I knew better. I knew in my bones that Rinaldo-Rolando-Renato played in that quaint, lovey-dovey scene a fatherly role; it didn't matter how she spun it.

❧

"Then, with the faintest splash," she told her father that evening, *"he disappeared underwater."* And yet my mother, from adolescent onward, told her father nothing more than an occasional neo-Victorian tidbit she had "read" (she invented most of them, frankly) in a women's magazine: "It is polite to remove your gloves delicately, one finger at a time"; or, "One oughtn't toot one's automobile horn at passersby—it is vulgar"; or, "For dark or puffy eyes, the most desirable variety of cucumber is the Lebanese." She abhorred such remarks, but continued producing them at the rate of about one a week because they seemed

to please him—he would lower his fork, his coffee mug, his newspaper, his penknife, his three fingers of bourbon, and fix her with an affectionate, crooked smile—which is, for a man of his generation, quite understandable: it's comforting to know your one and only daughter, even if owing to her embrace of the petty, old-timey conventions of our gender, needn't look very far, or indeed look at all, to find happiness. Though it was clearly one of the great regrets of her life, I never once looked down on my mother for this long-standing façade. Don't we all acquire some peculiar means by which to extract from our parents tiny drops— our fix—of love and affirmation? (I used to lie out my mother's dresses at night, pairing each with this or that stocking or high heel or scarf or bead necklace.) Don't our hearts plunge down to Aeneas in the underworld, failing three times to embrace the shade of his father, his arms grasping at nothingness, thin air? Sure. But a fairy tale does not in this sense explore relationships; rather, it is superficial, concerned with observable behavior. Just as a merman appears with neither explanation nor justification, so too does a daughter speak openly, unashamedly, to her father.

❀

Out of the corner of my eye, I saw a waitress, our usual thin-hipped pony-tailed waitress who would no doubt ask about my mother, approach. When she arrived tableside, greeting me with an informal "Hey" and the slightest gesture—was I imagining things?—toward the empty chair across from me, it was as though an immense shadow had overtaken me on a narrow sylvan road at midnight. I said nothing. I stared down, trying to bestow upon my notebook, white linen napkin and paper tablecloth the same heavy-lidded gaze my mother had bestowed upon her window. With her thick endearing accent, our—my—waitress asked, "You want usual?" and I was torn between slapping her in the mouth and weeping against her tiny, crimson-shirted breasts. Instead I nodded, then clapped shut the menu and thrust it into her hands.

Why do fairy tales omit such uncomfortable, coincidental, basically pointless moments that seem to comprise—I was in a cynical mood—the waitress staring down at me, waiting for either an apology or a thank you—half of one's life? At least fairy tales mention grief: indeed I feel, on that front, thoroughly represented. In "The Burial Shirt," which I'd encountered several months earlier, perusing fairybooks for a friend's baby shower on the slow-creaking, book-musty, second-story floor of Green Apple Books—in this tale, the ghost of a mother's seven-year-old son, holding his moon-pale shirt, sits at the foot of her bed and says: "Oh, mother, please stop crying, or I will not be able to fall asleep in my coffin, because my burial shirt will not dry out from your tears that keep falling on it." Presently our waitress left the table: the shadow slipped into the forest. Also, needless to say, I didn't buy my friend that book.

When my mother and grandfather began to speak openly to one another, when they had at last ripped open the reticent, over-mannered fabric of their relationship, it was too late: he was in a home, suffering from leukemia and dementia, and would repeat (as my mother rolled him in his wheelchair around the ultra-green, sprinkler-blossomed grounds) long-buried childhood stories. There was one in particular about a talent show. For weeks and weeks my grandfather had practiced in his slant-roofed attic bedroom, with its view of a church steeple and a solemn gray river, a tune called "Beer Barrel Polka," though in his mind he was on stage, he stood in celestial spotlight, a little unassuming ten-year-old with—what's that he's got there? a harmonica? a chromatic harmonica?—oh, boy, this oughtta be good. Then he would play, eyes squeezed shut, rocking back and forth on his heels, his encrimsoned cheeks alternately ballooning and shrinking, producing in his mind endless lush blue fields of sound, his entire body growing larger and larger, taller and taller, until, as though peering down the sheer hoar face of a mountain, he could see his audience—a silent black mass of insects—seated at his feet. "Well, that didn't happen," my grandfather would mutter, rolling under the Rorschach's shadow of a palm tree. She would touch his shoulder, and he would tilt his head so that his large cold ear pressed against the back of her hand. On the late November morning of the talent show, when his name was called, my young shaggy-headed grandfather walked across a dinky makeshift stage, stared out at the audience shifting in their seats, and instantly (dropping his harp, which resounded through the gymnasium) suffered his first and most serious asthma attack.

Could this experience alone have stoppered his dreams, his daydreams, his imagination? Turned his rich interior life overnight to stone? Seems unlikely. Yet to some degree it must have contributed to his eventual austere and reticent demeanor, to his fear of or inability to express his interiority, and maybe (who knows?) to his long and uneventful career as a bank teller. I suppose my grandfather was—being so consistent, so predictable, so utterly (as far as my mother could discern) unchanging—I suppose he was rather like a character in a fairy tale: a person for whom the passage of time arouses little if any change. In fairy tales, characters grow up, grow old, grow out their hair, their nails, their noses; their potbellies grow, their eyebrows (or a third eye) grow; out grow their boils. Nevertheless, their interior worlds, as well as the exterior worlds they inhabit (bucolic, crayon-drawn backdrops, for the most part), remain pretty much unchanged. I believed my mother—by some admixture of her father's personality and her own peculiar sensibility—must have felt like a child protagonist in a fairy tale: young, isolate, dreamy, inquisitive, beautiful, longhaired. Through her tales, I believed, she was trying to share with me a modest portion of that magic.

🌹

And at once I see her on the other side of the Klamath River, just standing there in an oversized yellow T-shirt and Birkenstocks, staring up at a small dark gap in the line of pine trees. See her morph into the girl from the fairy tale, then into a white-tailed doe who, turning her long neck in my direction, morphs once more back into my mother. Then she starts up the embankment toward the gap in the trees, where a wide shaded path curves into the distance; for a split second, on the lip of the embankment, she pauses, the breeze lifts her dark hair, and her chin rises as though following a scent. I'm up on my knees in our steel-blue Kmart tent, panicked, fourteen years old, watching her through mosquito netting. My mother, my lodestar. Where are you going? How long will you be gone?

🌹

Weeks later the girl brought home an oyster and told her father the merman had given it to her and said he would surface again when the oyster opened. Well, then, since nothing ever changes, there would be no need for my mother to have mentioned the sudden drop in sea level, allowing the girl to paddle clear out to the barnacled rock a quarter-mile from shore—a slice of cling-wrapped plum cake on the thwart across from her—and there for the first time unfold the long-ignored letter (at least she assumed it was a letter) her own mother had left for her on their pinewood table. But the girl began instead with the plum cake:

she set it on a flat of the rock and, crosslegged, with pursed lips, prayerfully pulled back the cling-wrap. Then she shoved half the cake into her mouth and just let the wind whoosh up the wrapper and fling it at once further and further, tiny and tinier, out over the bottle-green water. After a moment, as the crumbs tumbled down her shirtfront and into her lap, the fisherman's daughter unfolded the letter—or, wait, it wasn't a letter—it was a sketch, a pencil drawing—the very drawing, as luck would have it, that I'd once found under a rust-orange pouch of potpourri in my mother's sock drawer: a self-portrait in which the left eye, the right half of the nose, the upper lip, and the very tip of her Woolfian chin had all been so often sketched and erased, then sketched again and erased, and again sketched and then erased again, that the face was nothing but a tornadic lead-gray blur littered with eraser dust, a face disappearing behind a mask of smoke. And yet I supposed—as the other half of plum cake rose between thumb and forefinger toward the young girl's opening mouth—I supposed this was a fitting image. In fairy tales, certain family members (mothers in particular) are often altogether excised.

🌹

Looking up from my notebook, I saw before me a cheap metal teapot and an empty, willow-pattern teacup. How long had these been here? How had I failed to notice an actual human being traipse over and set them down?

🌹

Mystery, the unknown, is at the center of the fairy tale. That its reader-listeners must suspend their disbelief is a vulgar truism; far more interesting is the fact that they must suspend their desire to know what's omitted, what's hidden, so to speak, behind its teller's back. Can a fairy tale be restored, returned like a medieval painting to a previous compositional moment, a road not (or only briefly) taken? Can some bedandruffed Hungarian scholar please peel back this or that sentence like overpaint and reveal, behind a centuries-old boulder, say—though this is not at all the tenor of my mother's imagination, I realized, pouring myself a cup of tea—a jealous mermaid, pink coral dagger in hand, lying in wait? One must walk gingerly through a fairy tale; each step may detonate a new slew of questions. *The father, still unconvinced, lobbed the oyster into the fireplace.* Hence: Why is the father unconvinced? What is he unconvinced of—the existence of merfolk, or the merman's invitation to look for oysters? The adverb "still" implies that he's been unconvinced for some time, but have they discussed the matter, or has he kept his skepticism all to himself? (I could go on and on with such questions.) In any event, for the father to lob the oyster, seemingly without deliberation, into the fireplace, I thought it fair to presume that their relationship had incurred at least a minor fracture.

Then for a long time I stared out through the rain-pocked, misted-over picture windows, and remembered the mystery at the heart of *Citizen Kane*. After his second wife leaves him, the enraged and dying Charles Foster Kane destroys her ornate, over-furnished bedroom, but is suddenly calmed by the sight of a snow globe. He walks toward it. He picks it up. He utters the word "rosebud," and at that moment the little globe slips from his hand, bounces down a few stairs, and shatters. The remainder of the film is partially concerned with the mystery of that word. Rosebud. *Rosebud.* What could it possibly mean? Soon a nurse enters and, kneeling in the sharp-edged noirish shadows over Kane's dead body, crosses his arms upon his chest. In the film's final scene, Kane's childhood sled, on which the word "ROSEBUD" has been painted—a rather anticlimactic discovery, no?—is chucked into a blazing furnace, where it burns and burns...

I blinked. Orange rain fell slantwise in the lamplight. Cars and scooters and fixies shushed by. "I watched a rosebud very long," wrote Christina Rossetti.

🌹

"Rosebud" undoubtedly makes a gazillion such appearances. A favorite: The "Rose-bud," or "Bouton de Rose," is the name of a French whaling vessel briefly encountered in *Moby-Dick*—a ship that, in its quest for ambergris, drags along its flanks two dead sperm whales, as well as a thick, miles-wide cloud of "unsavory odor." ("Like a sweet-smelling flower in a coffin," wrote Nathaniel Hawthorne. My mother would love to know that Hawthorne's youngest daughter, Rose, was endearingly called Rosebud on account of her red hair.) But unless grief, too, emits an odor, unless I was right then stinking up Szechuan Gardens, I had no desire or patience to sniff these "rosebuds" out.

🌹

Sipping my tea, I thought principally of the first time I snuck out of my house (twelve years old, in the seventh grade) and hurried along pitch-dark back roads and narrow winding creekside paths to a boy's house; or, rather, to the small barred bedroom window of a boy's parents' apartment. I ought to have worn a red hood, to have carried a cake and a little pot of butter. I tapped on the glass. I leaned my head languidly against the cold bars. And when he appeared, bleary-eyed, tousle-haired, glancing back just once (stealthy, not scared) over his shoulder at his light-framed bedroom door, and eased open the prisonish window, I said—with naïve suavity that even now flushes my neck—I said: "Hey there, handsome." Beyond this, however, I don't remember much about that night. I remember only that he kept scurrying toward the door and listening for footfalls and motioning with his hands for me to duck my head—like a mock-frantic performance in a silent comedy—and that afterward I strutted home through the dark verily brimming with self-satisfaction, the night air cool on my skin, the owls hooting unseen overhead, and yet resigned absolutely to this absolute fact: I would be caught. I would turn the final corner onto our street and see, up ahead, in our half-curtained living room window, my mother staring daggers at me over a cup of scalded milk. Yet it was worth it, totally worth it, wasn't it? To sizzle with adrenaline, to fatten with pride, to glisten with hot-sticky accomplishment?

Years earlier still, making a wish (and I've always wished, like a proper Aristotelian, for happiness), I dropped an Eisenhower dollar down a well, then stood motionless, waiting for the coin to plink against the stone sides or else plop satisfyingly into the water. But the coin just dropped into blackness—just dropped down through a hole in the earth—no sound at all. When I'd turned at last onto our street, our house was full dark, my mother was no doubt snoring under her green-and-yellow afghan, and I felt again that hollow, heart-stopping disappointment: I realized I had wanted my mother to know how courageous (though she would certainly have favored the word "stupid") I had been. I'd wanted her to catch me, to punish me; I wanted to prove that I had not separated myself from her, that I was not like a Muisca chieftain who, washing away the anointed gold, glares around him at an empty shore, his onlookers vanished, a solitary white-bellied heron lifting off the pink water. For the first time in my life, a secret stood between us: my mother had not witnessed or known about, had not caught me at or followed behind a safe distance from, this most momentous of steps.

The waitress lowered a large serving bowl of wonton soup onto the center of our table. Then she set before me, beside my notebook, which I had upside-downed lest she spy my psychotic scrawling, a matching individual bowl and a Chinese soupspoon. With silent dignity (good-postured, chin high, the back of her small left hand pressed to the small of her back) she began to ladle the soup from the serving bowl to the individual bowl, and I at once regretted having taken—though there didn't seem to be, at the time, another option to take—a bewildered, wounded approach to our interactions. I should have pretended I was meeting my mother. After ten or so minutes of sitting there alone, I should have fished out my clamshell cellphone and pretended, a little too pixieishly perhaps, to talk to her: "No, it's fine, I totally understand . . . Yes, of course, you *will* make it up to me." I would laugh. "Talk to you soon. Feel better, okay? Ta-ta." Then I would sit there for all to see, a smile (or the ghost of a smile) still on my face as I clapped shut my cell and placed it back in my purse, knowing I had—or *had* had, to be precise—even grammar can inflict pain—a good mother.

Such a banal, imprecise description, "a good mother." Yet it seemed to bring her back: she perked up in the chair across from me, picked up her chopsticks and began to swipe them together as though sharpening knives—it's what she would do when the dumplings were served. But what was her cute, idiosyncratic tic for the serving of the soup? Something to do with the spoon, the napkin? I could not for the life of me remember. My good mother wasn't yet cold in the ground, and already she was disintegrating from my mind. I wanted to ask the waitress if she, returning the ladle now to the large bowl, remembered what my mother would do when the soup arrived. Then again, maybe we could just talk for a while, the waitress and I—a serious conversation between strangers—such things happened, right?—the way Chekhov's clerical student, after a hunting trip, when the temperature plummeted and the wind picked up, approached a pair of widows, mother and daughter, and commenced (warming his hands over their eerie, much-crackling fire) a conversation about the Apostle Peter: "'At just such a fire the Apostle Peter warmed himself,' said the student, stretching out his hands, 'so it must have been cold then, too. Ahh, what a terrible night it must have been, granny! An utterly dismal long night!'" The waitress, however, half-bowing, had already taken her leave.

I panicked. I cleared my throat in a grumpy, staff-beckoning way. Very quietly I whispered: "She's dead. My mother." Though the waitress continued walking, I believe I detected the subtlest hesitation in her gait, the subtlest turn of her head. Probably she had heard me clear my throat, nothing more, and preferred—rightfully—to be beckoned otherwise. Serves me right. (*You appreciate the pun, don't you, Mother?*) Still, I had reached out and been denied. I had made myself intimate and vulnerable and in need of help. And the waitress, strutting away, had tossed me into the fireplace.

🌹

A fairy tale is staunchly impersonal, if not ruthlessly cold: the tone is hardboiled, apathetic; the language is too simple; tragedy simply occurs; nothing about it is romantic or poetic or lyrical. *One morning the girl didn't get up out of bed.* Despite the fact that—or rather precisely *because*—the teller doesn't try to make the reader-listener feel even a pinch of sorrow, as is only proper, we feel impelled to rush to the girl's bedside, to fold her hands in our hands, to make up for the absence of authorial empathy with our own empathy. This is very different from a so-called "conventional" story whose teller attempts to make its reader-listener feel, or lead its reader-listener toward, emotion; in those stories, the teller is (we believe) guiding us through the tragedy, even if she has invented the tragedy in the first place and then made us its invisible witnesses, its attendant ghosts. But nobody's guiding us through the "real" world. So it must be true that fairy tales, despite their inherent marvelousness, sometimes more closely resemble life.

❦

When I entered my mother's apartment one late spring Thursday morning and received no response to my bushy-tailed tootleloo, there was neither frightening silence nor the high, suspensefully held note of a violin. I set on the kitchen counter the almond croissant from La Boulange (her favorite) of which I'd taken several surreptitious nibbles. Then I listened to the ever-so-faint squeal of the muted TV: a mounted cowboy squinted in the shadow of his hatbrim. I was certain my mother lay dead somewhere in the apartment, but did I hurry from room to room, as in a dream, calling and calling for her? Quite to the contrary. I stood for a long time blinking in the fluorescent light of the kitchen, holding my keys. Then I started toward the front door—I was going to leave, I can now admit—I was frankly too scared to face my mother's lifeless body—when the balcony door inched open in the breeze. No scent of pollen-laden air, no line of sunlight slanted across her faux Persian rug. I stepped out onto the balcony. I wiped my eyes with my sweatered forearm. Yet there she was, my mother, alive, leaning against the cast-iron railing in her white silk robe (which neither slithered in the breeze nor caught the light briefly), watching the passersby three stories below.

I touched her shoulder. Cold, bony. She seemed not to feel my hand, or to even know that I was standing there behind her, until she asked very quietly: "Do you think we know each other?"

"It's *me*. It's *me*, Mother," I said.

"Your grandfather never knew me. Not really." Her voice sounded dreamy, far away.

"Let's lie down for a bit."

"Very somber fellow, your grandfather," she said, peering over the rail and frowning at something down below. "Wore a black hat all the time. Have I told you that?" (*You have.*) "The brim was so huge and round and flat. It was like the rings of a planet." (*I know—you've told me a gazillion times.*) "He sat immensely straight, too. Straight as a Roman column." My arms were around her, hugging her almost, trying to guide her back inside. There was an unusual disparity between her physical weakness and her ability to talk. "Even at night," she said, "on the porch, listening to the radio in his shirtsleeves. Still wearing that hat."

I had managed to turn her around now. We took a step in tandem.

"He was a godhead," she continued, clinging to me. "Strangers thought he was a pastor, a snake-handler maybe." Her bathrobe slipped open, revealing her pale loose awful nakedness. I fumbled with the silk. "My boyfriend once saw him in the street and took off running, losing a brown loafer, the coward." She laughed breathily in my arms; then, as we crossed the threshold together, her voice grew once again faint and dreamy. "Do you think I could have talked to him?" she asked. "Do you think I could have spoken to such a man?"

(*No. You couldn't have spoken to him, Mother. And his loneliness was not your fault.*)

I ought to have uttered those words. But the language is too simple. I guided her—I said nothing. All the way back to her small, turquoise-curtained bedroom, I said nothing at all.

❀

At the end of a fairy tale, there is a slight, usually subtle turn—a volta, as the sonneteers say—as when the teller of "The Three

Kingdoms," a Russian fairy tale, suddenly peeks out from behind his curtain: ". . . and they began to live happily together and are still living. I was at their wedding and drank beer. The beer ran along my mustache but did not go into my mouth"—an indication that the teller was sober and is, I suppose, credible. Anyway, this turn must be slight, seeing as detail (which is not at all the domain of the fairy tale) is essential to a turn as elaborate as the now ubiquitous "plot twist." Too, this slight turn should echo, ring out, linger in its reader-listener's mind: it should haunt her. *The fisherman lumbered in and found the child dead, but looking very womanly.* Four days ago I found my mother in her lavender La-Z-boy in front of the TV—the cast of *Gilligan's Island* huddled (as the yellow credits rolled and the sea-chantey theme song yo-ho-hoed) on the Technicolor shore—a double glass of port spilled across her muumuued lap, so that she appeared to be sitting in a pool of blood (among other things). I already foresaw myself, months later, at a string-lighted porch party, telling some friends-of-friends that I thought for half a second she had committed *seppuku*, or else been "gut shot"—did I think that could be funny, or interesting, or sympathy-inducing?—where-upon, noticing their startled, offended, horrified expressions, I'd emit a nervous titter and instantly comment upon their blouses. I was haunted indeed.

❀

My mother, by her own account, handled the death of her father with far more aplomb. Late one night, on the near-empty 38 L, she turned to two teenaged girls buckled over with laughter at the back of the bus and said—as the neon lights of Geary Street played across her face and bunned-up hair and almost-teary eyes—she said, "Please stop laughing. My father has just passed," then continued to stare regally out of the rattling Plexiglas windows, turning up the collar of her black velvet coat.

Setting down my B-of-A pen, I watched a double braid of steam rise from the bowls. It was a subconscious attempt to make my mother's death more external: Clouds blackened with mourning. Brahms' requiem issuing from the highest windows. The flowers of Asphodel shrieking forth out of the asphalt-slathered earth. For better or worse, I never learned how to live without my mother, and so floundered, whereas she had learned to live without her father long ago. I already knew that I, alone in an elevator, or peeing in a public restroom, or standing in line at a hipster-filled Philz Coffee, would have no answers for the questions: How could the entire world just go on, business as usual, oblivious to or heedless of my mother's absence? How could she of all people just disappear? Just drop down through a hole in the earth, no sound at all?

Oh, yes, now I remember . . . When our waitress lowered the large bowl of wonton soup onto the center of the table, my mother would at once scoot it toward her with both hands and then, taking up the ladle as though it were a spoon, ask after *my* soup's whereabouts. She loved corny gags so much, and repeated her repertoire of them more and more as she aged, which, to my surprise, never embarrassed the hell out of me. There was in fact something perennially endearing—touching even—about them. Now, having set aside my notebook and small bowl of soup, I commenced to scoot toward me (not as a gag, but as a gesture of mourning) the larger serving bowl in which thronged wontons, bok choy, shrimp, thinly sliced pork, scallions, the caps of shitake mushrooms, as well as my own ever-so-slightly rippled face staring up at me. I cried quietly for a while. I sipped my tea. At some point, glancing up at the four card-playing waitresses, it occurred to me that nobody in a fairy tale reflects upon life; stares out over the ocean from a rock promontory; stands out on a balcony in her white silk robe; sits up panicked on her knees in a sunlit tent; gazes out of a rattling San Francisco bus or third-story bedroom window; slouches in a wheelchair remembering the stage on which he once stood as a ten-year-old, gripping a Hohner 64 chromatic harmonica. Reflection, remembrance, reminiscence, one's ever-deepening, ever-beckoning interiority— none of it exists. A fairy tale is all action. A fairy tale does not in this sense explore relationships. Even so, more useful than an artifact of reflection, I realized, lifting the Chinese spoon and staring back down at myself staring up at me in my soup, a fairy tale is—as my mother must have known—the loose ends of a wonton skin waving ghostily in the broth—a fairy tale is an artifact upon which to reflect ...

In memoriam D.G., 1930-2014

Variation on a Legend

"Our most illustrious gardens, cathedrals, waterfalls, stone angels and so forth," said the cabbie, leading us through the dark streets of the Tenderloin. I saw a man relieving himself under the caged light of a tenement building, and I gripped the sides of Stewart's little copper urn, seeing as I couldn't grip his hand. "Champagne, madam?" said the cabbie, raising a bottle. "No, thank you," I said, "—I'm in mourning." He steered with his knee, poured champagne into a flute, then handed it back to me. I saw a woman lean out of a high window, flapping a white sheet, and I drank instinctively. "Ahh, the scent of roast duck after a rainstorm," said the cabbie, stepping out at the next red light. I stroked Stewart's urn in my lap, as though I was stroking back his hair, soothing him, as I used to, after a nightmare. I could feel the faintest mist settling around my ankles, the red light leaning into my eyes. "How much farther to the Jacksonville Hotel?" I asked the cabbie. "Just over the drawbridge, madam," he said, crawling back in behind the wheel. The light turned green. The cab moved on. I saw a prostitute ethereally smoking under a neon-lit marquee, his brown skin flickering. When we pulled to the curb, it took me a moment to even see the place, so dark it was, so utterly black against the night sky. "I'm supposed to scatter my husband's ashes in there, in a fountain," I said. "I assumed as much, madam," he said, opening the door for me. "Thank you for the champagne," I said. "Please—it is our job to help you through this difficult time," he said. Out of the darkness behind me, I heard a distant scream, then an awful retching—like a bucket sloshing up a well—and I clutched Stew's urn to my chest. "I'm afraid of the dark," I said. "Well, I might suggest you lift your veil, then, madam," he said, reaching toward me. He lifted the veil, the darkness, from my face. I saw the sun breaking over the Jacksonville Hotel, a celestial outpouring over the picture windows, over the white façade, and

I stepped out of the cab. My mule stood waiting. Golden mule in the white sunlight. The cabbie hoisted me up. "To the fountain on a path of violet petals," he said, patting the animal's rump. "You've been very kind," I said. "Madam, your husband would be proud." He bowed. The mule shifted beneath me. I spent a moment balancing Stewart's urn up against the horn of the saddle, figuring we might as well enjoy this view together. Then I said, "Goodbye," and disappeared at a brisk trot.

In memoriam B.D., 1921-2011

Variation on a Fable

When Fannie and I moved to Chicago, to a spacious brick-and-mortar loft in the West Loop, I began to write a long series of nature poems. "Is everything all right?" she asked one evening, unpinning her long brown hair in the dresser mirror. "Oh, it's nothing," I said, "—a passing phase." I sat on my side of the bed, holding Rimbaud's *Illuminations*, admiring the way Fannie's hair curved down her back like the trunk of a cypress tree. I knew that it was not a phase, that even our spacious loft would sometimes suffocate me, but I didn't know how to break it to her. The next day I wandered the streets, barefooted, picking up seagull feathers, tapping the walking stick I'd whittled. "Fan," I imagined blurting out at the dinner table, "I'm a nature poet." Worst-case scenario, she'd choke on the skin of her baked potato and keel over. That would solve the problem, I suppose, except I knew I'd miss her: the dimple on her left buttock; the ever-tweaking arc of her thin eyebrows; even the hip, urban slang she liked to slip into our conversations. Overhead, the clouds disintegrated. I reached into my pocket and fondled the pebble I carried—a little black crumb from the Mesozoic era—and tried to center myself, despite the river of stroller-pushing mothers shoving past me. When I arrived back at our loft, I saw that my desk had been plundered: quills busted; ink pooled on the desktop; drawerfuls of nature poems scattered across the floor. Fannie sat in my wooden chair reading my logbook. "I suppose we should move to Montana, then," she said. "A stick-and-mud hut in the purple shade of a mountain." I said nothing. My heart fluttered. "White buffalo drinking from the moonlit waters," she read, standing. I took a step backward. Her voice fell to a whisper. "Fire crackling in a darkened wood. Dried plums and *The Flowers of Evil*." She had me backed into a corner. "Remembering Chopin, as the first light shatters through the spruce trees."

Variation on a Myth

[H]e going to bite her by the neck and then she got him.
—James Baldwin

1.

Many years ago, on his parents' back porch, listening to *The Marriage of Figaro* over Bloody Marys, J's mother (deep in the shade, languishingly drunk, wearing a broad-brimmed hat and rhinestone shades) suggested that he write a vampire novel. Ignoring his sudden, heavy-browed glare—J wrote detective novels and found the suggestion insulting—she craned her neck to better hear the Count's deep-voiced arrival, that famous scene in which Cherubino cowers behind Susanna's gilded chair, and it was then that he noticed, in the curve of his mother's long pale throat, the tiniest pair of teeth-marks. He set his Bloody Mary on the rattan patio table. *My father's body*, he thought, *isn't even underground—.* J stood, hollered over the music, "See you tomorrow, Ma!" and headed inside to fetch from the kitchen one of her many decorative garlands of garlic bulbs. His mother, head lolling, munching a celery stalk, raised one drunken arm, then fluttered her fingers at him. He ambled down the hall and, leiing himself with the garland, stepped into his parents' bedroom.

2.

Now, at his writing desk with a mug of coffee in the almost-pink dawn, his marriage failing, his mother and father three and seven years (respectively) gone, J remembers stepping into their bedroom. Quiet. Just muffled opera sounds. Remembers thinking: *Where shall I hide till evening?* In the far corner, under a mound of clothes, sat a purple velvet claw-footed chair, and he at once spotted, on the floor behind it, two faded black sockfeet peeping out. "I'm armed!" he had shouted. A lot of sudden breathing and squirming from behind the chair. Then, very slowly, his father rose up—face powdered white, hair pomaded back, wearing a black-and-red silk cape. J remembers he didn't have to say anything at all: his father simply lowered his white-gloved hands and began to talk. The whole stunt, he'd said, was for J's mother. Their marriage had grown miserable, well-nigh irreparable, from over a decade of neglect and nonpassion: if he struck up a conversation, she'd wander into a distant room; if he touched her, she'd snort and writhe and shoo him away. And at night, worst of all, he'd said, she would crawl into bed and turn her back to him and float away on a dream. J's father said he had to take drastic measures, life-or-death measures, you know, son? He said he knew she would miss him—and he was right, he added, raising a gloved forefinger—after he was dead.

3.

J blows the dust from the album, places it on the turntable, and lowers the needle into the groove. His wife, who also loves opera, first bonded with his mother over cheap sherry and a compilation of soprano arias, so when the overture (after a series of fizzles and pops, like warm RC Cola poured over ice) begins, J is in three places at the same time: in his parents' bedroom, in his current study, and on a rocking chair before the hideous lime-green sofa of his former B-Street duplex, where his mother and soon-to-be wife sat gabbing for the first time. He gazes down into his coffee (rippled surface, already cold) and wonders how, after watching the twin mascara-black tears runnel down his father's cheeks, after hiding the old "vampire" at his duplex for a few weeks— he'd later reinstall himself in the home—so he could lope across town in the middle of the night and slink through his mother's bedroom window and whip his cape over them, the two never happier, never (paradoxically) more alive—after all of that, J wonders, how can his own marriage, for almost precisely the same reasons, fall apart? But no: not precisely the same reasons; it's too neat. As a detective novelist, he should know better. He should know that his own marriage is nothing at all like his parents' marriage, that his wife, who dislikes children, who curses Tom Brokaw every weeknight, who still wears army-green Doc Martens and reminisces about the "hot girls" she slept with in college, so that at times his own sex feels vaguely incongruous, humiliating. He should know in his bones that his wife, despite her occasional maternal protectiveness of him—she once threw a fork at an agent in an uppity New York bistro for criticizing his first novel—is nothing at all like his mother. Just then, the first act begins: Figaro on his hands and knees measuring the space for a bridal bed. *My wife is sleeping*, J thinks, *in our own bridal bed—*. He slurps his coffee, remembers the night she trimmed his beard on the porch, grasping his entire head in her hands, checking for evenness. Remembers the afternoon they necked like nocturnal animals in the back of the grainily dark local theater showing (of all films) *Nosferatu*.

4.

J stares into their bathroom mirror. An assortment of makeup strewn across the counter. A black fur-lined cape curled catlike on the lino at his feet. He presses a little brush into a dish of talc powder and taps it with his ring finger, the way his mother used to ash her Virginia Slims. Then he leans toward the mirror, squinting at himself, and begins to dab his face.

The Domesticated Troubadour

he's too young for it now   the romantic posturing
on rain-   soaked terraces   & the distant sea
crashing   his kids are putting   clips in his hair
outer-space stickers   on his sunburst strat
now it's more than enough   to leap from cushion
to matte-gray cushion   avoiding carpet-lava
& calling for help across   minute distances   even when
he hauls out the garbage   past midnight   odor
of damp leaves in darkness   there is no inkling
of song in him   he's sure the romance will return
someday   in a sweep of cheatgrass   cloud-
shadows drifting   over his open palms   but then
where will his kids be   when again will he count
with eyes closed   or rise from among their sleeping
bodies   so quietly   he almost forgets
his ancient calling   almost forgets   to breathe

Little Boxes

Lost woman of Lilliput,
the witness, midwife to my agonies,

raised to the heavens,
most phlegmatic of mates,

I have trapped you
in one of Popa's little boxes—

but you only sit there crosslegged,
nibbling your fingernails,

a shoebox painted black
and purfled with many cottonballs.

stroking your tow-colored hair.
In the meantime, I am crouched

How lonesome it must be
to stand there all alone, to do nothing

in my ill-lit basement with one eye
narrowed in your moonhole,

but stare at this endless four-sided night . . .
With a butcher's knife,

listening to my wife's continuous
clopping footfalls overhead . . .

I poke tiny holes for stars, a larger hole
   for my blinkless eye—the moon.

Then I stand an Army Man inside,
   the one whose rifle is forever

"Just one more little box," I say,
   among an infinity of little boxes,

handing you one, which happens to be
   coffin-shaped and just your size.

Sleeping Lions

the willing giving over of the self to the other, to power
—Jack Halberstam

When I arrived, around noon, at the Blue Danube Café,
    A plump gentleman clambered up out of his pink chair
Begging me to take his seat, please, sit down, sit down.
    My feet tingled. "Splendid," I said. Another large man
Began to take my arms out of my coat. "Ahead of time,
    As usual," said a petite woman, seated across from me,
Lifting her demitasse. She seemed to resemble a figure
    From my deepest past. A hand was placed on my knee.
A pale hand on my dark trousers. A girl, in front of me,
    Asking me what I should like to order. "Coffee, strong,"
I said. A faint, meaningful light haunted the blank wall
    Behind the counter. A woman beside the petite woman
Said: "Oh, dear, you must be tired," and, indeed, I was

    Half asleep. My mother hung above me, tucking me in,
Pulling the white sheet up over my face. "I'm fatigued,"
    I told the woman, though she had long since moved on
To wittier conversation. "How ambitious he used to be,"
    Said a young chap staring down at me. "What a waste,"
His friend agreed. In a circular mirror, on the side wall,
    The whitest snow fell. My porcelain cup of cold coffee
Sloshed about in my lap as if I was driving somewhere
    To the din of battle drums. Still, I was courteously still.
"He seems, well, *excited*," said a tanned young woman,
    Coming right up to my face. A couple of bookish boys
Stood watching. "I wouldn't do that," one of them said,
    Grimacing. "No," said the other. "I think that's enough."

Intermezzo: A Fairy Tale?

He has already traveled (privately) much farther
Than even the boy in his young wife's favorite novel
   Who returns from Yu Province clutching a heap
Of blue silk which, as he strides into town, rivers out
   Behind him, making everyone for a split second
Lean against her rake or pop his head through a bead
   Curtain, unaware that in a late, haunting chapter

This will shroud his mother's body and shudderingly
   Reflect her ring of candles. Yet he, the actual he,
Not the boy in the novel, creeps home empty-handed
   Through the elongated shadows of their banister
Every Friday afternoon, wanting his mauve armchair
   Before the awning window, where he can watch
The quiet rain fall. And here he is watching the quiet

Rain fall through the linden trees and onto a girl
Loping down the street, her yellow heels in one hand.
   Whereas he admires such flamboyance in others,
He prefers to sit alone under a languorous ceiling fan
   And to shove his mind out over the brick houses
Like a boat. His single flamboyant gesture: marrying
   A woman half (or nearly) his age who, suffering

From vertigo, lounges about in humungous tank tops
   Rereading paperbacks or repeating one-fingered
Melodies, as she is now, on their vaguely out-of-tune
   Kawai, letting the sound echo through the house
And into his dark imagination in which she imagines
   He is imprisoning her, Rapunzel-like, in a tower
Over a moat of blue glass reflecting her many suitors

Fastened like insects round the round stone wall.
To sit beside her again, on the piano bench, plunking
   A few simple well-timed chords to her melodies,
He will pretend not to have traveled but to have been

Right here, all along, her dense, night-black hair
Pooled across his shoulder where one of her little sea-
   Shell ears is nestled. The travel makes him exist

On a crowded street in Kyoto, wagging a panama hat
   Against the odor of fish booths and hosed-down
Cement; he cannot project himself onto a silver plain
   Where he can (lying flat) observe the monstrous
Loam-dark underbellies of grazing buffalo, an image
   He encountered years ago in an adventure novel
Found in an ill-lit motel, even if their entire marriage

   Is built on such projections: both of them facing
Their shade-smeared backyard after an early matinee
   In which three boys pricked each other's fingers
Then joined a torch-led procession of hooded figures
   Along a monochromatic beach, whose waveless
Black water ripples, now, over their wind-tilted lawn . . .
   Thus they have remained together, or separately

Together, for almost a decade; their minds have been
   The torches their empty bodies, without moving,
Followed. Now see him follow her childish melodies
   Through the quiet rain, and strike the jade-green
Bell of the sky, as up he tugs himself out of the chair
   And starts downstairs trailing his own faux river
Of blue silk. Now see him bend over her at the piano,

   Passionate restraint personified and set to music,
Where she is reading and noodling on the white keys
   All at the same time. Gorgeous sad-eyed woman,
Whom he will never deserve, sitting among shadows
   In a sienna wood at sundown. He will touch you.
He must touch you. (His hands doubled in the ebony
   Gloss of the piano.) Touch you and feel *real light*—

Voyage Out (2)

My sister's creative, more than creative than I, though less creative than my brother, whose creativity I sometimes believe must be an act. Just this morning, for example, I watched him slip into his backpack the C- English paper he'd hung by a length of string from our carport all semester, planning to turn it in, he told me, now that it was browned and wrinkled and torn in places, like three treasure maps stapled together, as a "rewrite." And yet my sister, whose creativity I never question, is no doubt the likelier *poseur*, being a charter member of the Cinemaniacs (a club that watches and squabbles over films) and herself an impassioned method actor. Once, for a whole month, she floated from room to room in a peach-colored maiden's gown, speaking to invisible interlocutors in an angelic, barely audible British accent. Well, maybe they're both acting—they're teenagers. You can imagine, I'm sure, how difficult it is to live with them; too much creativity can be a liability: not every occasion calls for shoving a black fishnet stocking into the horn of our old Victrola, even if it does make Prokofiev sound a bit naughtier. Tonight, like every night for the last month, I have plopped down on our brown leather sofa (afghan draped around my shoulders, bowl of movie-butter popcorn in my lap) to watch reruns—the most un- or anti-creative thing I can imagine. All the time I feel my sister and brother stare down at me from the landing of our staircase, as though from a rain-soaked dock, while I unmoor my little sofa-shaped boat. They are, I am certain, waiting for some long-overdue creative outpouring. Why else would they be so quiet? *Fine. Let them sigh,* I tell myself. *Let them grip the banister, let them whisper vulturously among themselves.* Having no more use for creativity than for, say, an encyclopedia of modern chess openings, I now simply let myself drift away into the make-believe mist over the make-believe water, sockfeet propped on our leather cushions, chuckling to an episode of *M*A*S*H*.

Nocturne

late   in the unlighted hospital room
remembering that night   his wife hitched home
through the dark   cradling their dead goose
in her arms   & Brahms rustled
on the phonograph   he looks outside now
where the rain is hammering as it was hammering
that night forty years ago: *the door creaked open*
the candleflames leaned against the wind   & she
drifted in   weeping   sopping wet   letting the goose
in its green wool blanket   tumble to the floor
he can hear the piano now too   Intermezzo in B-
Flat Minor   settling at that moment on the tonic
yes: *settling*   his wife is dying in the next room   her heart is in some-
body's hands   tubes enter her   & here he is
on the edge of the bed   remembering their dead goose
he expected more   like reciting Popa together   on the porch
or long walks   through the mists of Muir Woods
twigs cracking underboot   in the blue chair
in the Brahmsian dark   a small mound of flowers
O deceitful flowers   lavish   reeking
of rat pellets   this must not be happening   & indeed
it is not: when he blinks   the streetlamps flicker
in the lot   raising his right hand   the red fern in the corner un-
furls its fronds   there's no ground beneath him   no
ceiling overhead   now he too is sopping wet:
black cloak over the goose   candles on either side
clutching his wife to his chest   in the quivering light

at the head of the dining table   she is leaving him
after forty-two years   now he will try rising
from the edge of the bed   but of course there's
no rising with-   out holding her

Here and Not Elsewhere. Thus and
Not Otherwise

To have become, us three, in the Viennese room, an ensemble—
    Was that possible, was that me,
                  undressing in the olive-green light, for example,

While you stood in the kitchen, on pointe, listening to *Norma*,
    Our aging priestess, in your golden leotard?
                         I am embellishing again, investing

The past with so many niceties, so much romance, when time,
    In fact, has left nothing
                except rain on your skin / the evening you pirouetted in,

Naked under your black trench coat, singing our "Casta Diva"—
    And there I go again: embellishing, embellishing . . .
                      Your little calloused feet

In my ordinary hands—is that corrupted, is that me, kneading
    The arches, the heels, the curled pink toes,
                      while our ancient Victrola crackles

Under the paper lantern? To have opposed the cold, all winter,
    With our reckless bodies, the sheets slipping under me,

70

our most desperate aria

Climaxing: a picture accurate enough, it seems to me, though
    It is invented, therefore uninhabitable,
               like a bedroom at the bottom of the sea.

Here are the three windows: square, uncurtained, one for each;
    There is the wet street wandering toward the *Stephansdom*,
              only to circle back

To the Viennese room: to you, in your square window, pliéing
    To our opera, our soprano
         walking with her lover, hand in hand, into the pyre—

Could I sense the flames, could I simply stand there gripping
    My leather shoulder bag crammed with records,
           ready to leave, to never return?

The thought is laughable; no doubt a dramatic embellishment—
    I stand behind you / rubbing a knot in your shoulder,
             sneaking down the leotard

To better dig in my knuckles, until the inevitable end appears:
    Me, unpinning your hair, on the needlepoint stool,
           while the priestess calls to us

Across the room, ahh, tremulous fluttering: and you turn to me—

Desire Lines

I place my hand in the small of your back—
A smooth, flesh-colored bowl
                                        I once filled with water
And drank from, in dusk-light, like a deer
In the quiet center of a forest—so that when you speak,
    When your response to my childish claim
That the world could be burning
                                        and I'd still be happy—
    I see us, briefly, amid falling volcanic ash
And black leaves, naked, all set to repopulate the earth—
    Is, simply, half turning round to study me:
"But I love the world"—well, then,
                                        my hand vibrates,
    Your voice in the quiet center of my hand
Vibrates and crescendoes and then courses through me
    Like a spirit singing through the long, red-
Carpeted halls of my body,
                                and all my vague idealism
    About us as two lovers, tucked in shadow
In a pool of ferns under a private moon in a lyric poem,
    Has if not disappeared—you're still there,
After all, trembling above me,
                                        aqueous and moon-pale—
    Then at least deteriorated, photodegraded
By the late, eucalyptus-scented, summer morning light
    Of your skin, here, *right here*, at the head
Of our bed
                that now rises, behind curtained windows,
    In a quiet uncurtained corner of the world
Amid a field of flowers, human-faced, opening for you—
    The two of us, each with an inward flame
Burning on the red,
                        rose petal-strewn altar of the other,
    Made public now, together, made to exist
In full view beside or under or on top of or deep inside

One another, dawn after wet purple dawn,
The sheets shushing like a faint shore under us—

                                 thus—

Desire Palette

He was reading. Then
The shadow of the pine tree
Brushed across the page.

He set the book down
When the shadow of her hair
Brushed across the page

Is it her shadow
Or the shadow of the pine
That darkens his page?

Is he holding Proust?
Will the shadow of her hair
Brush across *Swann's Way?*

Desire, he thought,
As the shadow of her hair
Spills across his thigh.

Reading in the nude,
The shadow of his love's hair
Brushed across his page.

His love's hair's shadow
Spread across the open book
In his hardened lap.

Oh, forget the book:
The shadow of his love's hair
Brushed his naked thigh.

Then he spends himself
On the shadow of her hair
Upon the white page

"White clouds, white stones." Then
The shadow of his love's hair
Spills across the words.

To touch the fine words
As the shadow of her hair
Spills across his page

On page 56,
The shadow of his love's hair—
A revelation.

Did he *pine* for her
As the shadow of the pine
Spread across the page?

No shadows, no book—
Just his dull pencil drawing
Her charcoal-black hair.

Words will mean nothing
Once the shadow of her hair
Sweeps across this page

Landscape with Martyr

Afterward, he watched her lumber out of the coliseum
    Swinging the severed head of his panther—

All that talk about Madrid and his old Segovia albums
    And look what good it did them. Outside,

In the pomegranate dusk, she flung the panther's head
    Into the sidecar of her sepia '57 Triumph

And roared, her orange hair flapping, into the distance.
    Remember the mirror over their pine bed

In Ohio, loving her double nakedness night after night
    With the snow falling? His mind escaped

Into that fragrant, still-warm profusion of white sheets
    And denied (kissing her ears) the present

Wherein he stood at the ironwork gate of the coliseum
    Watching her panther's tail of black dust

Settle over the stone field. (Touching her arched spine,
    Listening to the fizzle of the phonograph

In the static winter dark.) Later, restored to the present,
    He would lug his headless cat to a furrier

And make of it a coat, luxurious, with abalone buttons;
    In the meantime, he alternated his mouth

Between one tamarind nipple and the other, expecting
    A little talk, afterward, about the beaches

Outside Valencia. *Ribbons of spume in the lapis water,*
    Clam boats pitching in the diamond light—

Then he watched, in real time again, her Triumph melt
   Into the mercurial horizon. It was crucial,

He felt, to attend the final scene. Raising his right arm,
   He told the spectators to go home. Listen

To Segovia. Eat dinner. Keep your roses to yourselves.

Fermata

He had imagined himself onto the edge
  Of a great precipice. Wind and woodwinds,

White light and the smell of fawn hides

  Over the olive stones. Sometimes a woman
Soaping her testicles in the purple rapids,

  Greater even than Coltrane playing Chopin

On the soprano sax. He had had his life
  In the Russian Hill apartment, shooting her

Among the cartons of Chinese take-out

  And in the tangled orange sheets of his bed . . .
Feeling her lips on the back of his neck

  Each new morning, and peering over at her

Just to be sure. He had made it through
  Like a man teetering in darkness, thrusting

His hands into unidentifiable pots, then

  Smearing the contents over his naked body.
Now he was content to watch the goats

  Graze in the hot scrubland. The young boy

Chiseling a serpent into his maple flute . . .
  Understanding Monk's instinct to abandon

His piano, his quartet, in Charlie's solo,

Just so he can dance. The sound of absence
Will outdo one's sound. Still, he dances—

In memoriam, J.G., 1925 – 2012

Littoral Couplets

first sweat
  then glitter

beneath her
  i was an orb

of vapor slow-
  dissolving

bari sax
  for sunrise

double bass for
  humid nights

she wailed
  across the moon-

lit waters
  like a ship

once
  in a salt cave

i licked
  a wall until my

tongue bled
  the dawn rose

at the nape
  of her neck

later
  in the crushed

mica
  on my chest

she traced
  a cabin

hum for me
  she whispered

the ballad
  on the gramo-

phone inside
  often then

i sensed her
  in darkness

sheared my
  white hair

the shore's scent
  the ship's wail

i hurled my
  shadow upon

her shadow
  in the sand

Acting, Method (2)

In Cork, Ireland, I stopped at this little cottage-like restaurant
    And there sat Homer, all alone, hunkered over a bowl of stew.

I wanted to introduce myself but, at the time, I wasn't myself.
    A huge sailor hat gripped my head and I couldn't lift a teacup

With this ghastly hook. "If it won't ruin the afternoon," I said
    To the waitress, "I'll have some tea and a godforsaken menu."

Homer sat there glaring at me with ferocious, glass-blue eyes.
    His enormous spoon hovered, dripping, halfway to his mouth.

Grandpa had been neglectful but he taught me never to lower
    My gaze. I clenched my one good hand. I could stare forever.

Like prison inmates at lunchtime, I lifted my hook to the light,
    He petted the limp pheasant's head in his sack under the table.

Round Midnight (3)

Hotel sign in Greece:
Clytemnestra's Inn. With Bath.
"Let's get outta here."

Sleeping Lions (2)

Evenings, in the damp grass under the folding table.
   Were you grappling with your loneliness, even then,
Little plastic sword across your lap?
                       The pine trees
   Rustled in the darkness; the Coleman lantern hissed.
I remember. I would tap my father's workboot, then
   One calloused hand would descend, pinching a scrap
Of porkmeat.
            My mother would skim her bare feet
   Over the grass. Hours, watching the shadows dance
In the turnip garden, listening on the TV to the war
   In Iraq. *But they had made a space for you: a chair,*
A placemat. Once, against the chain-link fence, I sat
   Reading Aeschylus,
                 ignoring their bellowing at me,
Hot blood spurting from Agamemnon's neck. Rain
   Brought us together again: beneath a dripping eve.
Did you believe you'd find something—
                   a little soul—
Deep within? Mornings, and the gray lambs bleated
In the silence, in the mist. I lay under our dark coats
   In the closet, my mind flittering from empty sleeve
To empty sleeve . . .

Our Pillar

Our son toddled around
In my *Moby-Dick* shirt. Our daughter
Was a bruise-colored blanket
Tumbling from her bed to the floor.
We gathered stuffed animals
In our arms, or we took turns
Spacing out in front of the coffee-
maker. I wrote a poem
About a green ribbon falling
From an egret's beak. One minute
We heard them snoring to
Earth, Wind & Fire; the next
They were squatting on our chests
And gnawing slobberingly
At our fingers. You say,
They meow at sunset, they ooze like mist
Across our floors, they definitely
Have wings. One of them locked us
In the bathroom, the other
Busted us right out. We were
Archaeologists searching for a fabled
Wooden block. Our hands
Glided side by side into the
Darkness under the sofa
Like swans. Remember the end
Of Kafka's "The Bucket Rider"
When the narrator *ascends*
Into the regions of the ice mountains
And is lost forever? Our daughter
Pointed down the hall, to a path
Of floral-print cushions . . .

Lineage: 7 Variations

1.

My grandmother's alone, more alone than I, though less alone than my grandfather, who lives in a hut back of our house—like Tolstoy—and who I sometimes believe must have a secret family tucked away in a little ruined port town, where he goes when he needs to talk to somebody, or squeeze somebody's hand, or just stand beside somebody on a creaky, barnacled pier stretching out to sea. Even so, my grandmother, who never leaves our attic and whose love for absolute solitude I never question, may likelier possess a secret family: sometimes, late afternoons, practicing my cello in the tan hills overlooking our house, I'll see an arm fling out of her tiny circular window—a signal that she's hungry—but is it really her arm every time? She could have an entire other family up there, and I (holding a high note, climactic, heavy vibrato, in the citrus-scented shade of a lemon tree) could be responding to somebody else's arm. You can imagine, maybe, how difficult it is to live with them: unsheeted beds, empty fiddle-backed chairs, spotless placemats, the wind lifting the blue curtains. Would you even believe I stalked a family last night—mother, father, two boys, a girl—into a café, into the gelato parlor, then through the lamp-lighted park and down a narrow, bark-chipped path and to the lake, where I at once darted away like a skittish deer under the pinery? I had the sudden, cold-sweat feeling that my grandparents, in my absence, needed my company: my grandfather on the porch tuning his fiddle, or my grandmother folding back my comforter, all set to tuck me in. But could I ever reach them, could I ever burst into our house in time? Let me tell you: the silence, when I arrived, was deafening. I gazed up at the starlight; I did not dare go inside. Too afraid to face such solitude, too fragile to be let down, I tromped round to the side of the house—yellow porch-swing cushion shoved under my arm—then dropped down through the black hole of the storm cellar, where sometimes I'll spend the night.

2.

When it begins to exist for others it ceases to live in us.
—Arthur Schopenhauer

You've been so quiet, so much quieter than I, even if you're still less quiet than your father, whose only sound each evening, as he puffs on his after-dinner cigar, lost in a reverie of woolly smoke, like a mountaintop, is a long belch-like groan of satisfaction. Still, we hear things at night (the pop of a cork, a chair scraped back) and believe, lying upstairs in the dark, that you must be talking to somebody, leaning in close, giving away all your secrets. In fact we worry that you'll soon have no private life at all, no warm interior space in which to hide, as a ground squirrel hides— *needs* to hide—under frozen earth, wrapped in its thin tail. And then, tell me, what will you do? You will wander the brick streets looking for others' secrets, for the quietest people, as though you could hide (and you cannot hide) inside them. Maybe the best way to protect you is to show you, here, now, in this letter, that language contains innumerable trapdoors: the word *pebble* is uttered, and at once you're standing on the bank of a sunset-smeared river littered with white funerary petals, squeezing my pinkie finger, and talking about how the water gurgled over stone, or what one decrepit woman whispered, or why you could not look at the red-faced men sobbing and gripping their hatbrims—so that a secret, a private feeling, however minuscule or trivial, is now outside of you, now an object that strangers can lift and peer into, the way a monstrous eye can fill a dollhouse window. Would you even believe that last night, because I heard (as your father's belly quietly rose and fell) nothing at all, I tiptoed downstairs and out of the house and from shadow to shadow, my wine-colored bathrobe streaming be- hind me, slunk toward the louder neighborhoods, expecting to find you? Quite soon, behind a corner maple, I spotted a man I used to know, before I'd met your father, chatting with a young woman (not you, thank goodness) outside a Moroccan restaurant, no doubt exchanging some exotic-breathed secrets en route to a cinematic kiss, and I realized that I could, after all these years, still taste the salt on his lips, still feel his thick mahogany hair (now flecked with silver) between my fingers, still hear him breathe—pant almost—right in my ear. I didn't love him, this older man, this onetime Assistant Professor ("Ass Prof," he used to quip) of Cultural Anthropology, yet he activated something inside of me (an exuberance, a verbosity) that your father, who I nevertheless love eternally, seemed to shut down. Ohh, it is so quiet in our house, in our bedroom—only the faint scratching of my pen as I write by candlelight at our rolltop desk, like a monastic scribe. Indeed, listening to the sharp ring of silence, I suddenly believe that you are sound asleep, you are your father's daughter, and I am the odd, unquiet one who hears things and gives away secrets and in the quiet center of the night must scribble in her little lavender notebook, sighing. Maybe I should thank you for surrounding me with such quietness; then again, maybe my quietness is the best expression of my gratitude. Thus, as quiet as this candleflame, as quiet as my tall empty glass of milk reflecting the candleflame in our dresser mirror across the room, I'll slip into bed, and I'll pull the gauzy covers up over my voice and body. *Gute Nacht*, my daughter. You may not hear from me for a long time.

3.

My early stories are action-packed, more action-packed than
(as one friend, swirling wine with half-closed eyes, put it) my
"reflective middle period," but less action-packed than my current
stories, which are chockfull of car chases, explosions, shootouts,
swordfights, wild sex, the works. Still, I admire the naïve, even
vulgar, audacity of my early stories: lead characters tumble down
elevator shafts or vanish in snowstorms, their Oldsmobiles idling
bluely on the sides of roads. Now sensible reasons underlie all
of my decisions—my pencils are ruminatively teeth-marked—so
that the *action* of writing is, despite the excitement on the page,
rather unexciting. At this very moment, in fact, gazing out from
my study window at the dark birch woods across our road, I
consider the weapons (dagger, derringer, throwing star) most
quickly secreted into a leather boot, and I grow nostalgic for my
middle period: the woods are so much more meaningful, more
mysterious, than little (or big) weapons; I ought to stand before
the darkness in my red silk dragon-print kimono, imagining this
or that character sloughing through leaves and underbrush, loping
over rocks and fallen branches, hacking with a machete through
ancient emerald vines, drawn inexorably toward a moon-silvered
chalice from which he or she (throwing off an enormous hiking
pack) would drink- deep amber wine dribbling down his beard
or between her breasts—and sink at last into a deep amber sleep
wherein his or her entire life, soft-edged, in slow-motion, begins
once more amid the quiet birch trees . . . Or something like that.
The inescapable problem of such stories, the reason I stopped
pursuing them, is that nothing outside of a character's mind
actually happens; the virtual supplants reality; the reader,
twice removed, is like a woman watching a woman watch an
autobiographical film at the back of an empty theatre, dust motes
floating celestially in the projector's beam—a woman who will,
I now imagine, walk home in the rain in her light brown flesh-
colored stockings under a lemon-yellow umbrella thinking about

her life, about her film, pausing for a spell before an illuminated bakery window to follow with her eyes the glistening braided swirls of cinnamon rolls and Danishes. But where, dear reader, is the action in that? My life is already actionless enough. Pick up a book. Write. Take a snoozer. Watch a sitcom. Whip up a stir-fry in my tattered sockfeet. Hence, my stories are action-packed: the woman will enter their bedroom, find her husband's face buried between the deep amber asscheeks of a housemaid, and in a shriekingly dissonant instant of mindless rage reach down into her bootleg and grasp her derringer—I'm right now gripping my pencil over a blank page as though it too were a weapon, as though I too could inflict pain—and raise it and fire pointblank into their chests in quick succession: first the husband, who flails backward, still erect, spouting blood from his neck, and then the maid, who simply crumples to the floor like a dropped trench coat (with a blood-red rose in its lapel). Yet it occurs to me now that both action and "reflection" are, at root, just two different ways of searching for the same—well, *something*. I can go downtown and carelessly or methodically search for it in the smoke-filled, neon-lighted bars; or else I can sit up here at my desk and, slurping my cold sour metallic coffee, search for it in the mind. What difference does it make, finally? Ohh, hell, it makes a world of difference: reflection cannot poach my eggs, for example; neither can action interpret or examine or at all comprehend any other action, like the late June night in which I, after a sublime blues concert, clambered with a bunch of strangers into a graffitied, black-windowed sedan. Perhaps my stories, my *late* stories, will cease their searching altogether—as Kafka once said: "My stories are a kind of closing one's eyes"—and instead center around the derringer in the bootleg, moonlight trickling through the birch leaves, wine in the chalice, nothing at all on the page, dust or darkness or silence, faint piano music from another room, faint wind billowing the curtains, the blood pooling over the rustic pinewood floor, seeping into the crevices, into the fibers, seeping deep down into the earth.

4.

I'm handsome—a bit handsomer, I think, than my brother—but perhaps not quite as handsome as our father, whose dark eyes and delicate brushstrokes of gray about his ears make him look dignified and private—like a great exiled European poet—though he is in fact rather gregarious and clumsy. Just this morning, for example, emptying the dishwasher in his V-neck Hanes, a plate slipped from his hands and shattered instantly on the marble tile, an accident we'd witnessed a gazillion times: he stares down at the shards, nostrils flared, arms flung out, underlip angled grotesquely rightward, as though snagged on a fishhook. I must admit that he looks at such times (that is to say frequently) quite ugly—not at all as handsome as outsiders believe—which makes me, whose handsomeness is never marred by actions, the actual handsomest man of the household, don't you think? Still, whenever I look at my brother, who ought now to envy me and watch me, the way the two of us long envied and watched our father, he is gazing at himself in a gilded mirror, or a storefront window, or a bottle-green puddle out back, so that I think that he (with his crew cut and tight black tees) may indeed be the handsomest, and that I have little sense of my own appearance, or of my very self—inside or out. Now, at dusk, I reach into the kitchen trashcan, lift out a shard of broken plate, and hold it up to my face, as I'd seen somebody do in a tragic opera: my left eye, funhouse-mirrored, stares back at me dimly, disfiguredly. But I refuse to look away; I feel certain that my brother and our father are, from their respective doorframes, silhouetted behind and on either side of me, waiting for me to renounce myself, to slam the shard back into the trashcan, and to—why else would they be so quiet?—slink away into the shadows, an ashamed monster. Thus I continue to gaze at myself, thus I begin to sway from side to side in the dusk-lighted kitchen, running my free hand through my hair. My handsomeness, I must admit, seems not to matter at all anymore. As long as I keep up this performance, as long as I keep them silhouetted in their doors . . .

5.

Yesterday is so boring, don't you think?
—David St. John

Yesterday is so boring, so much more boring than tomorrow, though not quite so boring as today, don't you think? Today I trudged out to that little bus stop at the edge of town, where I once passed a woman paring mushrooms in a yellow nightie, but the place was desolate: the shadow of an immense condor wheeled before me in the dust. At least yesterday I sat beside my aunt in her wheelchair on the sparkling convalescent lawn, nodding and looking off and slurping coffee from a Styrofoam cup, even if she didn't speak to me, but only stared out from under her heavy lashes, like a cow, which can be so boring. And yet tomorrow—tomorrow I may at last, in the watery predawn silence of my bedroom, sense a presence so cold and unseen hovering above me, waiting for me to enter it like a man thrust into nothingness, into silence, whereafter yesterday and today and even tomorrow will have all become so boring, don't you think? Well, I think so, and I feel so, too, almost as though tomorrow is in fact today, and I am hovering in the starless night above a blazing bonfire: boys drinking with the firelight in their teeth; girls dancing in circles, jiggling music from their silver earrings. Still, the idea of now prodding this mental picture for meaning, whether today or tomorrow or even yesterday, is frankly so boring, too, don't you think? I belong down there in the dust, kicking Coke cans, whacking things with sticks. Chucking rocks at telephone wires. I mean, for Chrissake, how did I even get myself up here—an invisible sailor in an invisible crow's nest—with the sky so dark and the sea stretching out so calm and boring over almost everything?

6.

A people's dress tells one a great deal more about them than their poetry.
—Henri Michaux

Our grandfather's brown flannel suits tell us a great deal more about him than his poetry, more about him even than his tastes in music—polka and Dixieland and gypsy swing, nothing else—though maybe less about him than his gestures, which are as rehearsed and grandiloquent as an old silent tragedian's. Today, for example, when my sister and I rang his bell after school, he promptly swung open the screen, clapped his heels together, lifted his chin, and, very butler-like, swept one arm toward his darkened, fusty-smelling interior. In his starched shirt and blue-and yellow-striped tie, he looked non-retired, a man still at the office crunching numbers or making sales calls, still married to our rosacea-cheeked grandmother who, chain-smoking Capri Super Slims, refurbished antique dressers on their back porch—nothing at all like the retired widower bent just seconds ago over a poem (*my body like a tamarind on a branch . . .*) in his study, listening to the Hot Fives. I realized, in fact, that our grandfather's suits are rather misleading. Because of them, he is mistaken for part of a community, one of many brown flannel suit-wearers, as opposed to what he is: an *isolato*, on the fringes of even his own family, which may incidentally account for the grandiloquence of his gestures. If he felt close to us, would his arms, after escorting us into his living room, really dart and waggle over his leather sofa, as though playing stride and boogie on the keys, beckoning us to sit? He soon popped *King Kong* into the VCR, gave us each a Klondike bar—an afterschool ritual—and then retreated down the shag-carpeted hall and into his study. We never stayed more than fifteen minutes.

Now, at dusk, walking the winding creekside paths behind his neighborhood, running our fingertips along the brown flannel pads of cattails, I wonder, too, whether he would have, if he felt close to us, any desire at all to write poetry; to

93

perpetually address with a dull pencil his late-lamented "you" (car accident, on her way to Raley's for asparagus and eggs); to grasp as it were at nothingness, page after empty half-page—a disembodied gesture, no less grandiloquent—in the presence of actual flesh and blood. The writing of poems is no doubt a lonely enterprise, and lonelier still to write them in such a public, upper-middle-class uniform. (I always imagine poets draped in heavy robes.) Still, the scratchy music issuing from our grandfather's old Victrola in the corner of his study, causing his neighbors to slam shut their windows or, after midnight, swing open their shutters and bark at him to *turn it down for Chrissake*, announces his isolation, creates around him an impenetrable enclosure, a carapace of brass and reed improvisation. Right now, however, Django and Grappelli are playing (quite softly, too), and my sister and I, peeking over his back fence, tippy-toed on the sun-bleached plastic milk crates that Hmong fishermen use for stools on Sunday mornings, see our grandfather standing among antique dressers on his back porch, just looking out over the green sea of his overgrown yard. Suddenly he plucks from the ceramic ashtray one of a gazillion stale accordioned cigarette butts, which he then presses counterclockwise against his lips, smearing ash, and after a minute places it a little erotically, a lot Eucharistically, on his outstretched tongue, an image he may later insert into a poem (*whoever is bereaved enough to eat the past . . .*).

I watch him as one might watch a memory in a crystal ball through a telescope in a silent movie, as though I am already much older, looking back—maybe leaning against a pillar on my own back porch, blowing the steam over a mug of black coffee—and now at last understand the pain implicit in, and seeping odorously out of, his flannel suits and gestures, his poetry and tastes in music. No attribute is more telling, finally, than any other. Yet we are, my sister and I, mere children: we haven't the means or the desire to comprehend, much less breach, the old man's self-protected psyche. What do we make of his blank, heavy-lidded face now gazing straight ahead, swallowing the cigarette butt? *Not much*, I tell myself, as we pitch the milk crates back toward the edge of the creek, and though a little corner of my heart wants to stay, we start together up the dirt path. *Nothing worth thinking about at all, really.* And indeed the scene is already nothing more than a brief, impromptu stop on our way to our cousin's, where we will eat Pringles and fruit snacks; where we will construct an enormous room-sized fort out of sheets and afghans, chairs and cardboard boxes; where we will crawl on our bellies through dark narrow tunnels, scarcely breathing, trying so hard not to be found.

7.

My father's a very fine musician—a better musician, at least, than my uncle, who will strum his guitar and croon to old wide-hipped ladies in the subway, like a troubadour—though he's not nearly as fine a musician as my wife, out of whose centuries-old violin rises warm rich earthy phrases, as redolent as the steam of mushroom soup issuing from a cottage. And yet, last night, when I heard (tugging our little King Charles Spaniel around the block) ever so faintly in the still air the third movement of Bartók's *Sonata for Solo Violin*, I thought only of those long mauve childhood summer evenings in which, walking home from a friend's house, I would hear my father playing trumpet in our living room—luring me the way feral cats are lured toward singing—so that the memory of his horn (regardless of quality) actually supplanted my wife's violin, and I was for half a second a child again: baggy red windbreaker, weird alien dog at my feet. How could my wife, even with her extraordinary talents, compete with *that*, the very sound of my childhood? Well, as it turns out, with Rachmaninoff's *Vocalise*, which my uncle will hum in falsetto at family barbecues, tossing onions on the grill, and which my wife is right now playing in our bedroom as I lie across our bed in white cotton briefs, arms behind my head, as though she should—and she can—snake-charm my member. Though my father's playing can do nothing (thank goodness) of the sort—the sound of a trumpet in fact repelled my mother and has done little, in her decade-and-a-half-long absence, to attract a surrogate—my uncle's deep, syrupy voice has no doubt flushed a few women's cheeks in its time. Possibly, then, a gazillion people have fallen under the spell of my wife's violin: I wonder how many neighbors are sprawled across their own beds, letting her music pour in over them through their open windows, like peasants being showered with coins, and I wonder how I have come to be—implausibly—the one allowed to behold her (and the spider-dance of her fingers) here in our dusk-lighted bedroom, listening to her as one might listen to a message on a phonograph during a rainstorm through a walkie-talkie, a secret I cannot quite discern. Am I not therefore a deficient partner, incapable of understanding, much less responding to, my wife's deepest communications? I belong in my father's living room, or riding the subway with my uncle; I am still, deep down, the nine-year-old who falls asleep to a cassette of lullabies (instead of Chopin's *Nocturnes*). My wife deserves, in other words, a better listener—a *trained* listener—even if nobody's more willing than I to throw himself at her feet, to massage her neck after rehearsals, to soak her hands and wrists in warm olive oil and lemon juice. Indeed, I have already stood and am now, not unlike our little King Charles, kneeling at her feet—a ridiculous attention-getting trick, very effective: it receives a brief, knowing smirk—as her music (climactic, heavy vibrato) streams forth celestially overhead, like an aurora. I must admit I am quite comfortable here beneath her, in my tighty-whities, arms and legs outspread. Who would believe I do not belong here, that within her music is not contained my father's trumpet, my uncle's guitar and voice? Perhaps *that* is the static-glittery secret of my wife's music: her deepest communications are, in truth, my deepest memories: when the tonic swells in the arch of her ring finger, it swells from the past, it swells from the kitchen table at which I sat poking cold string beans, craning my neck toward the dark tunnelish hall, at the end of which I could see my mother, as through a fisheye lens, stuffing things into a suitcase—which is to say my wife is the finest musician because she has found me, her muse, her carpet angel of inspiration, while my father lost his (if he'd ever found it) fifteen years ago, and my uncle finds his wrongly, frivolously, each and every day. Now our blue- and green-striped curtains rustle, *Vocalise* is concluding, and my wife sways a little, closed-eyed, threading the long final note into silence, into still air . . . Already my entire naked chest has flushed with panic, as though her music, my memories, my family, are leaving us forever, though of course there will be—she lowers her violin and her bow—other performances, many others, as many as meals in a lifetime, private or otherwise, that pull me out of myself, that pull me back in.

Notes

Epigraph: The Woolf quotation is from *The Voyage Out* (1915).

Page 9: The Furukawa epigraph is from his novella *Slow Boat* (2017), trans. David Boyd.

Page 11: "I see only forms that are lit up and forms that are not"—a quotation long attributed to Goya (trans. unknown)—first appeared in French biographer Laurent Matheron's *Goya* (1858) and was transcribed, according to Robert Hughes's *Goya* (2003), from "overheard conversation."

Page 12: "6." is written after Kawabata's "Harbor Town," in *Palm-of-the-Hand Stories* (1988), trans. Lane Dunlap and J. Martin Holman.

Page 15: "I'm greener than the grass is green" is a variation of a line of Sappho's fragment 31 ("Paler than summer grass," trans. Sherod Santos) with a not-so-subtle nod to Robert Lowell's "imitation" of the fragment, "Three Letters to Anaktoria," in *Imitations* (1961): "I am greener than the greenest green grass!"

Page 30: "*Art thou a little spirit bearing up a corpse?*" is a corruption of a well-known Epictetus quotation recorded in Marcus Aurelius's *Meditations*: "Thou art a little soul bearing about a corpse," trans. Hastings Crossley.

Page 36: The Jackson epigraph is from his poem "Kind of Blue," in *Scattered Clouds: New & Selected Poems* (2019). The story itself is indebted to Kate Bernheimer's essay "Fairy Tale Is Form, Form Is Fairy Tale," in *The Writer's Notebook: Craft Essays from Tin House* (2009), where I first encountered Ralph Manheim's translation of "The Rosebud":

> There was once a poor woman who had two little girls. The youngest was sent to the forest every day to gather wood. Once when she had gone a long way before finding any, a beautiful little child appeared who helped her to pick up

the wood and carried it home for her. Then in a twinkling he vanished. The little girl told her mother, but the mother wouldn't believe her. Then one day she brought home a rosebud and told her mother the beautiful child had given it to her and said he would come again when the rosebud opened. The mother put the rosebud in water. One morning the little girl didn't get up out of bed. The mother went and found the child dead, but looking very lovely. The rose had opened that same morning.

Page 41: The quotation from "The Burial Shirt" appears in *The Complete Grimm's Fairy Tales* (1812), trans. Margaret Hunt.

Page 46: The Hawthorne quotation is from his short story "Edward Fane's Rosebud," in *Twice-Told Tales* (1837). The Rossetti quotation—the opening line of her poem "Symbols"— first appeared in her novella *Maude: A Story for Girls* (1897).

Pages 48/49: The Chekhov quotation is from his short story "The Student," in *The Witch and Other Stories* (1918), trans. Constance Garnett.

Pages 51/52: The quotation from "The Three Kingdoms" appears in *Russian Fairy Tales* (1975), trans. Norbert Guterman.

Page 58: The Baldwin epigraph is from *If Beale Street Could Talk* (1974).

Page 64: The Halberstam epigraph is a partial definition of "radical passivity," a term coined in his *The Queer Art of Failure* (2011).

Page 62: "Popa's little boxes" refers to Serbian poet Vasko Popa's serial poem "The Little Box." "*[T]he witness, midwife to my agonies*" is a phrase plucked from Book Four of Virgil's *The Aeneid*, trans. Robert Fagles.

Page 85: The Kafka quotation is a corruption of the final sentence of his short story "The Bucket Rider," in *The Great Wall of China* (1931), trans. Edwin and Willa Muir: "And with that I ascend into the regions of the ice mountains and am lost forever."

Page 87: The Schopenhauer quotation is from his essay "On Authorship and Style," in *Essays of Schopenhauer* (1890), trans. Rudolf Dircks.

Page 90: The Kafka quotation is from Gustav Janouch's *Conversations with Kafka* (1951), trans. Goronwy Rees.

Page 92: The St. John epigraph is from the opening chapter-poem of *The Face: A Novella in Verse* (2004).

Page 93: The Michaux epigraph is from *A Barbarian in Asia* (1933), trans. Sylvia Beach.

Acknowledgements

Many thanks to the editors of the following publications in which these poems and prose texts (some with different titles, some in slightly different form) first appeared: *Anthropocene, Barn Owl Review, Bellevue Literary Review, Blue Mesa Review, The Carolina Quarterly, Cerise Press, The Collagist, The Common, december, Cosmonauts Avenue, Devil's Lake, Drunken Boat, Fairy Tale Review, Free State Review, Fringe, The Hollins Critic, Inch, Memorious, the minnesota review, The National Poetry Review, Oxidant\Engine*'s BoxSet Series (2018), *Palette Poetry, Pear Noir!, Poet Lore, Popshot Quarterly, Puerto del Sol, Vinyl Poetry, West Branch,* and *Whiskey Island.*

"Desire Lines" also appeared in *Best New Poets 2015*, edited by Tracy K. Smith.

Some poems and prose texts appeared in limited-edition chapbooks: *The Rosebud Variations: And Other Variations* (Greying Ghost Press); *In Whose Hand the Light Expires* (Yellow Flag Press); and *Out, Voyage* (Broken Sleep Books).

LAY OUT YOUR UNREST